God's Workshop

*Meditations from everyday life
for everyday people*

May God bless you richly in you journey of life. Ps. 119:105

Joseph H. Housepian

GOD's WORKSHOP

Meditations From Everyday Life
For Everyday People

JOSEPH HOVSEP HOVSEPIAN

Belleville, Ontario, Canada

GOD'S WORKSHOP
Copyright © 2001, Joseph Hovsep Hovsepian

All Rights Reserved. No part of this publication may be reproduced, stored in a retrieval system or transmitted in any form or by any means – electronic, mechanical, photocopy, recording or any other – except for brief quotations in printed reviews, without the prior permission of the author.

Cover Design by: George Toufexis
Edited by: Ann-Margret Hovsepian

ISBN: 1-55306-259-0

All Scripture quotations are taken from the *New International Version* of the Bible (Copyright © 1973, 1978, 1984 International Bible Society. Used by permission of Zondervan Bible Publishers.)

"No One Understands Like Jesus" © 1952, renewed 1980 by John W. Peterson Music Company. All rights reserved. Used by permission.

For more information or to order additional copies, please contact:

Good News Ministries
5945 Park Avenue
Montreal, Quebec H2V 4H4
Phone (Canada & USA): 1-888-909-9626
Electronic mail: goodnewsministries@canada.com

Essence Publishing is a Christian Book Publisher dedicated to furthering the work of Christ through the written word. *Guardian Books* is an imprint of *Essence Publishing*. For more information, contact:

44 Moira Street West, Belleville, Ontario, Canada K8P 1S3.
Phone: 1-800-238-6376. Fax: (613) 962-3055.
E-mail: info@essencegroup.com
Internet: www.essencegroup.com

To the glory of God;

To my father Vartevar and mother Ovsanna, who gave me physical life, loved me, led me to Jesus and were the best Christian examples for me to follow;

To my wife Hasmig (Jessie)—God's choice for my travel companion in my life's journey—for being a faithful team-mate and godly wife, mother and grand-mother;

And to my daughters Ruth and Ann-Margret, for their love toward their parents and God, for their faithfulness and devotion to the ministry, and for teaching me how to be a father.

Table of Contents

Acknowledgements 13
Forewords 15
Introduction 19

PART ONE: Bought at a Price

In My Workshop 25
In God's Workshop 26
Hope for the Hopeless 28
Your Soul Is Priceless 30
Treasures in Jars of Clay 31
The Power of God 33
Which Door? 35
My Good Samaritan 37
Why Wait? 39
Keeping the Law 41
Your Life-and-Death Decision 42
Who Is Jesus? 44
Good News of Great Importance 47
The Glory of the Lord 48
Immanuel 50
  Coffee Break ~ What Will You Give? 53
"Behold! I Stand at the Door and Knock!" 54
Metamorphosis 55

Emptiness 57
What Are You Searching for? 59
 Coffee Break ~ Stop Searching. 62
Guilty!. 63
Caught in the Act! 64
Jesus Anointed by a Sinner 66
Unconfessed Sin 67
True Repentance 68
Forgiveness 71
The Joy of Forgiveness. 73
 Coffee Break ~ A New Year—A New Page 75
One More Year 76
Healing 77
Who Can Solve Our Problems?. 79
Is Death the End? 81
Our Soul Is Immortal. 83
Eternity 85

PART TWO: Shaped by the Master's Hand

A Strange Marriage 89
Committed or Gone Fishing?. 90
Wanted: Full-time, Permanent Christians 92
Keep the Words. 94
Grow in Grace. 96
Are You Growing?. 98
Growth Is a Must. 99
Marks of Maturity 101
With Wings as Eagles. 103
Power, Love and Discipline 105

The Journey of Life	107
Walk in the Light	109
Don't Look Back!.	110
Three Kinds of People	112
The Believer's Life	114
Hindrances to Faith	117
Peace	118
Good Works?	120
What Is Your Goal?	122
Obey or Not Obey?	124
"That's All I Want!"	126
The Vanity of Pleasure	129
Whose Side Are We On?	131
Jesus Reached the Helpless	133
Prayer	134
Itching Ears	136
It's Easy	137
Good Health	139
Pulled in Two Directions	140
True Happiness	141
True Prosperity	143
When Life Gives You Lemons	144
Do You Suffer as a Christian?	147
Life Is Worth Living!	149
"If Only"	151
Evil Times	152
Let Us Go On	154
Disappointed and Disillusioned?	155
Anxiety and Worry	157

Direct Prayer Line 158
Joy and Peace. 160
Why Do I Keep Stumbling?. 162
Holiness. 163
Are You without Sin?. 164
Be Clean 166
Cut It Off!. 168
Christ or Satan?. 169
"We Don't Need More Entertainment" 171
Avoid the Fruitless Deeds of Darkness 173
The Sin of the Heart 174
Sin Is Sin (no matter what you call it). 176
No One Understands Like Jesus. 177
Love—the Most Effective Tool 179
Honouring Mothers 181
What Is Love? 183

PART THREE: Refined Like Silver

Rend Your Heart 187
Sinners Saved by Grace! 188
True Religion. 190
God Hates Religion, Too! 192
 Coffee Break ~ Religion vs. Christ 195
Religion Does Not Save—Christ Does. 196
What Can Satisfy Our Thirst? 197
The Experiment Failed 199
Watch Out for Counterfeits! 201
Busy—but We Can't Fool God 203
Will a Man Rob God? 204

Jesus Saw	206
Jesus Has Everything to Do with It!	207
Is Christ Divided?	209
The Unknown God	210
The Church Must Be an Oasis	212
The Going, Growing Church	214
Why Does the Church Exist?	217
"What's in It for Me?"	219
The Church	220
Why Attend Church?	222
Woe to the Shepherds!	224
Christian Unity	226
The Hold-Up	228
We Are Not Alone	230
The Christian and the Occult	233
Spiritual Separation	234
Power over Satan	236
The Real Enemy	239
Revival!	241
The Valley of Dry Bones	242
You've Been Warned!	244
Why?	246
Invite Them to Church	247
"We Found Him!"	248
Coffee Break ~ Just a Spark	251
Not Me, Lord	252
The New Life	254
Good News	255
Scripture Reading Index	257

Acknowledgements

Although there have been many who have helped me learn, grow and mature spiritually—and this process will continue until I am called Home—there are two brothers who have been my mentors and who have helped and encouraged me to start and continue the ministries I am involved with.

Evangelist, author, broadcaster and a great missionary, **John Ertsos** is a beloved family friend whom I have known since my childhood. He is, in my opinion, what every servant should be. With his life and example he has taught me how to live and serve as a Christian. My special thanks to John and his wife Helen for their ministry and support.

Dr. Paul Stevens is a great friend, teacher and mentor. I met him and his wife Gail when I immigrated to Canada in 1960. He was the pastor of Temple Baptist Church and, although I did not speak English, he encouraged me to get involved in the church. A short time later he asked me to teach and preach. Paul has never stopped encouraging and mentoring me. His godly life has been a good example to follow. Thank you, Paul and Gail, for your love and support.

Forewords

"Life is a journey." So begins one of Joseph Hovsepian's brief but meaty meditations. And so it is—a journey in which the deepest questions we ask and the most pressing issues of direction and destination have to do with our souls. God made us for Himself and our hearts are restless until they rest in God—as St. Augustine said centuries ago. What Hovsepian does time and again is to show us how the God-shaped vacuum in our soul can be filled and how to live the faith.

These meditations are personal. They deal with our relationship with God. They do so by exploring the basics of the Christian faith—the Good News of Jesus, the unconditional love of God, forgiveness, sin and holiness. This is no watered-down version of the faith. People today are often inoculated with mild doses of religion that have made them immune from the real thing. The real thing is what these meditations are all about. Read them yourself as a daily devotion. Give them to a seeking friend. They represent a lifetime of teaching and writing by Pastor Hovsepian.

Inevitably, when people read a book they try to discover the person behind the words. It has been my privilege to know Joseph Hovsepian for almost forty years. I was once his pastor and have, over the years, watched him grow as a disciple of Jesus. He pastors a multi-ethnic church in Montreal, Temple Baptist Church. He also pastors from his electronic repair shop on Park Avenue, a business through which he supports himself and his family. Like Aquila and Priscilla in the Bible, Joseph and Jessie Hovsepian are tentmaking (self-supporting) servants of

God. I have lived in their home and vouch for their integrity—
a matter of no mean significance in an age of religious hucksterism. Both the man and the message are the real thing. So read. Enjoy. Believe. And thrive in the journey of faith.

Dr. R. Paul Stevens,
David J. Brown Professor of Marketplace
Theology and Leadership, Regent College, Vancouver, B.C.

*T*his book is full of messages that reflect Joseph Hovsepian's everyday experiences with Christ.

As pastor of Temple Baptist Church since 1984, and previously an elder there for more than twenty years, his ministry has been unusual. He speaks and preaches in English, Greek and Armenian, and also speaks French and Turkish. He is one of God's few workers who can serve in such a diverse ministry. Joseph has been a layman and pastor, relying on his business for his income; an evangelist; a radio broadcaster; a counsellor, both in face-to-face situations and on the phone; a servant in other ministries (such as my own, Gospel Reach-out Inc.) and much more. And now, a book publisher!

I have known Joseph since his childhood and I remember, since he came to Christ at the age of twelve, his great zeal to serve his fellow man for Christ. As a youth, he wrote and circulated Greek evangelistic leaflets. In later years, he wrote "What Are You Searching for?" (see page 59) and nearly one million copies have been printed (in English, French and Greek) and distributed around the world.

Joseph has a brilliant intellect, a highly trained mind and an outstanding gift of preaching and teaching. His great success lies in his consuming devotion to the Lord, his reliance on the Holy Spirit and his absolute trust in the revelation of God through the Scriptures. His messages are full of spiritual discernment and address the subjects of salvation, evangelism, the Christian life, spiritual warfare and, especially, the most desperately needed message in our churches today: revival at any cost. Many times Joseph's articles have given me ideas and outlines for the preparation of my own messages.

As you read this book, my prayer is that God will ignite in you a spark that will become a flame of righteousness and holiness in your life. Besides, this is the need of the hour as He is coming again. I hope you agree.

John Ertsos,
Evangelist

Introduction

How She Found Peace

She was about twenty years old. Although one of her legs had been amputated before she was even eight years old, she was determined to do well in life. She was beautiful, healthy and had already started her own business. But deep inside her heart she felt empty. Something was missing… nothing gave her the joy she was searching for. There were admirers, proposing marriage, but even that did not impress her much.

The bookkeeper at her father's brick factory, a poor young man, gave her a book to read. It was the Bible. One day, feeling empty and joyless, she took the book and went to the beach, which was less than a mile from her home.

She started reading and, although she was a God-fearing person and had practised her religion faithfully, she could not understand much of what she read. Then she came across a short portion that got her attention. She read it over and over again. Then she read it out loud:

> *For God so loved the world that he gave his one and only Son, that whoever believes in him shall not perish but have eternal life.* (John 3:16)

Tears poured down her cheeks. She fell to the ground and, with all her strength, she cried out, "God, heavenly Father, thank You for loving me so much. Thank You for sending your Son to save me, too. God, forgive me, the sinner. I promise to serve You for the rest of my life."

She got up and said, "God, I love You more than anything or anyone else in the world. Please, Jesus, take my life and my all and be my Lord."

She returned home a new person. She removed all her jewellery and gathered whatever she thought was worldly or vain and got rid of them. Then she ran to her mother and told her that she had found what she was searching for: peace, joy and life. She could not keep the wonderful news to herself. She shared it with everyone she met.

Eventually she told those who were interested in her and the man who wanted to marry her that she was a new person and that her life was going to be lived for Jesus, her Lord and Saviour.

Not long after her conversion, she was married to the bookkeeper who had given her the Bible. He was a born-again believer who was anxious to share the gospel with all those who would listen. They became a wonderful team and were blessed with two children, four grandchildren and three great-grandchildren. Her husband died in 1995. He was a faithful servant who served his Lord until his last breath.

Her testimony always starts something like this: "It was not at a crusade or at a revival meeting, nor even at a church. And, no, it was not even someone showing me the way to Jesus. I was saved on a lonely beach. I was searching for God and God was there to be found. He took my empty life and gave me a new one, a wonderful life, full of excitement. He can do the same for you too."

She is eighty-six years old today and still serving her Lord. She has a prayer ministry going all day—two telephone lines ringing all the time, with people calling her to pray with them over the telephone. She still is excited about her Lord.

You may have already guessed that this woman is my mother—my teacher, my friend and one of the prayer warriors who daily pray for my ministry and for me.

Do you think the believer's life is not exciting, that God does not answer prayer? If you could speak to my mother, Ovsanna (Hosanna), you would see that her excitement of serving the Lord, instead of decreasing, grows by the hour.

Are you experiencing the joy of your salvation? I hope you are!

Joseph Hovsep Hovsepian

Editor's Note

*I*t seems fitting to follow this tribute to the author's mother with some words from his daughter.

The legacy of incredible faith and dedication to Jesus Christ, passed on from my grandparents, generation to generation, is awesome. This spiritual inheritance has included a profound desire to share the Good News of salvation through Jesus Christ with those around us. And that's the call my father has been responding to for the past forty years or so—from his electronics workshop, from the church pulpit and, more recently, over radio air waves.

This book reflects a life spent in God's workshop, both as a clay jar (2 Corinthians 4:7) and as a tool (Proverbs 27:17). It is a sample collection of his sermons, articles and radio messages, and even a few of his poems (highlighted as "Coffee Breaks" in Part One and Part Three).

After a number of people suggested that my father compile these meditations into a book, encouraging him to share his insights with a larger audience, he prayed about it and decided that God was indeed calling him to publish this book. And at last, after a lot of hard work, here it is.

The book is divided into three sections, following a Christian's progress through "God's Workshop": our redemption and salvation through His grace, our spiritual growth as He works on and shapes our lives, and our deeper maturity as He refines us through our Christian service and through the challenges we face. Each meditation has a suggested Scripture reading and can be used as a daily devotional.

It has been a wonderful privilege for me to work on this book and my prayer is that you will be as inspired and encouraged by these devotionals as I was while I read and proofread and read them again!

Ann-Margret Hovsepian

Note About Attributions:

These meditations, as already stated, have been collected from many years of Joseph Hovsepian's ministry and most of his original sources are now unknown. He acknowledges and apologizes that there are a few quotations or references for which no source or credit is provided.

Bought at a Price

"You were bought at a price...."

(1 Corinthians 7:23)

In My Workshop

Reading: Ephesians 2:1-10

One of the things I do in my electronics workshop is restore new and old equipment. Sometimes a customer will bring in an old radio—defective and broken, with signs of wear and tear, and covered with dirt and tar—and say, "I don't know whether or not you can do anything with this radio. I found it in the lane near some garbage. Can you restore and save it? I don't want to throw it away."

My usual answer is, "Yes, of course I can restore it. That's my job." Then I add, "If you are willing to pay the price, I am willing to save it."

Restoring these old, broken and dirty radios is not easy, nor is it pleasant, as I often say to my wife, but somebody has to do it! Besides, and more importantly, restoring things that seem useless gives me a lot of pleasure. When the defective parts are repaired and the interior and exterior of the radio are cleaned, something wonderful takes place. The broken and rejected radio becomes a useful and beautiful piece of art because someone cared enough to pick it up and pay the price for its restoration.

If restoring a radio can bring so much joy, imagine what happens when a broken and rejected human being is found, cleansed, restored and saved. Jesus said:

> "There will be more rejoicing in heaven over one sinner who repents than ninety-nine righteous persons who do not need to repent." (Luke 15:7)

Jesus is the Restorer and Saviour.

For the Son of Man came to seek and to save what was lost. (Luke 19:10)

Asaph, the great songwriter, cried out:

Restore us, O Lord Almighty; make your face shine upon us, that we may be saved. (Psalm 80:19)

In God's Workshop
Reading: Psalm 51:1-12

One Sunday morning, as I was greeting people coming into the church, I noticed a man standing by the door, reluctant to come in. He seemed drunk or under the influence of drugs and gave the impression that he had not been washed or groomed for some time. When I went to greet him, he said he had just come to see the church. The man returned the following Sunday and, after a short conversation, he left.

He came once again, this time clean and sober. He started to tell me about the mess he was in: his life was ruined, not only by alcohol and drugs, but also by immorality and perversion in his life.

He came to church again, wanting to be "restored". He wanted a new life and was willing to pay the price. After confessing his sins and asking God to forgive and save him, he asked Jesus Christ into his heart to be his Lord. A miracle took place. He became a new, born-again person. He shone from top to bottom.

Later, this man was baptized and he joined the church, serving faithfully until he moved away from the city.

This is only one example of the many restorations I have seen take place in God's "workshop". Broken and ruined lives have been mended and saved. Empty and joyless hearts have been filled with peace and purpose.

God is in the business of fixing, mending, restoring and saving lives—not rejecting and destroying them. Jesus said:

> *"Come to me, all you who are weary and burdened, and I will give you rest."* (Matthew 11:28)

King David was a broken man, soiled with sin. He had lost his joy and was wasting away spiritually, emotionally and physically. He had lost all hope… until he remembered God's workshop. He ran to God and cried out:

> *Have mercy on me, O God, according to your unfailing love; according to your great compassion blot out my transgressions. Wash away all my iniquity and cleanse me from my sin…. Restore to me the joy of your salvation and grant me a willing spirit, to sustain me.* (Psalm 51:1-2,12)

In my workshop, I restore broken and discarded radios to make them last a little longer. In God's workshop, He restores broken and rejected souls and gives them eternal life.

Because God restored me, too, in His workshop and gave me a new, meaningful and eternal life, I am compelled to spread the Good News that God's workshop is open for business twenty-four hours a day, for as long as there is time.

Have you been to God's workshop yet? I hope you have!

Hope for the Hopeless
Reading: Mark 5:21-34

Do you ever feel hopeless? Even if you aren't poor, sick or lonely, you probably have felt hopelessness at some time in your life.

King Solomon was one of the richest and wisest people in the world and he was constantly surrounded by people. Even so, we see his real despair at one point:

> *So I hated life, because the work that is done under the sun was grievous to me. All of it is meaningless, a chasing after the wind... So my heart began to despair over all my toilsome labor under the sun.* (Ecclesiastes 2:17,20)

Solomon felt so empty that he exclaimed, "Meaningless! Meaningless! Everything is meaningless!" (Ecclesiastes 12:8).

Hopelessness is one of the major problems that people face today. It is usually a result of personal or family problems, the world's political, environmental and economic situations, and crime. Governments and people everywhere are lost, helplessly waiting for some leader or group to do something.

Many people will tell you that they have given up all hope. Hopelessness is like a contagious disease: unless it is stopped and reversed, it spreads all around.

Many people have lost the will to live. Why? There are many different reasons, but the Bible points to godlessness and disobedience. Apostle Paul wrote to the Christians in Ephesus:

> *Remember that at that time you were separate from*

> *Christ... without hope and without God in the world.* (Ephesians 2:12)

God's warning is loud and clear:

> *However, if you do not obey the Lord your God and do not carefully follow all his commands and decrees I am giving you today, all these curses will come upon you and overtake you: You will live in constant suspense, filled with dread both night and day, never sure of your life. In the morning you will say, "If only it were evening!" and in the evening, "If only it were morning!"—because of the terror that will fill your hears and the sights that your eyes will see.* (Deuteronomy 28:15,66-67)

Doesn't that passage perfectly describe people today? Is there a way out of this hopelessness? Yes! God has promised that,

> *... all blessings will come upon us and accompany us if we obey the Lord our God.* (Deuteronomy 28:2)

Jesus also promised:

> *"If anyone is thirsty, let him come to me and drink. Whoever believes in me, as the Scripture has said, streams of living water will flow from within him."* (John 7:37-38)

Jesus is the Water of Life—the only hope! Many don't understand or believe that, but those who come to Him in faith will find peace, hope and healing. A good example, in Mark 5, is a woman that Jesus healed. In faith she touched Jesus... she didn't just crowd around Him like everyone else. Touching Him transformed her life. Finally, she couldn't keep her transformation a secret.

This woman's hopelessness disappeared after her encounter with Christ. Yours can, too. Jesus may not change your situation, but He will change you! He can heal you today.

Your Soul Is Priceless

Reading: Psalm 8

To the person who does not believe in God, the idea of an eternal soul and God's interest in man may seem absurd.

Someone once said: "To believe that there is a God who created the human race and gave each person a unique eternal soul, which will continue to live forever either in God's presence or cut off from him and suffering forever, is absolutely unbelievable and beyond human understanding."

Well, this person was right. To believe that there is a Creator who not only created us and sustains us, but also has a deep personal interest in us and loves each one of us is, humanly speaking, illogical and contrary to reason. Yet that is exactly what the gospel is all about!

The Bible clearly says that the only living God created us in His image.

> *Then God said, "Let us make man in our image, in our likeness...." So God created man in His own image, in the image of God He created him; male and female He created them.* (Genesis 1:26-27)

And then we see Jesus paying the price of our redemption.

> *For all have sinned and fall short of the glory of God, and are justified freely by his grace through the redemption that came by Christ Jesus.* (Romans 3:23-24)

The question is: "Who are we after all, that God should care for us?" The Psalmist asked the same question:

> *When I consider your heavens... what is man that you*

are mindful of him, and the son of man that you care for him? (Psalm 8:3-4)

When we look at it through Christ's eyes, we see that He values us even though we are sinners. Our worth comes from God. We, on our own, have nothing to offer in return for our salvation and God's love. He cares because we are made in His own image and His breath is in us. God proved His love for us when He gave His one and only Son so that whoever believes in Him will not perish, but have eternal life.

This might sound foolish or absurd to the unbeliever, but God knows the value of each soul and the cross is proof of that. Apostle Paul wrote to the believers in Corinth the following:

> *For the message of the cross is foolishness to those who are perishing, but to us who are being saved it is the power of God.* (1 Corinthians 1:18)

Dear reader, your soul is priceless. Remember the price Jesus paid to redeem it.

Treasures in Jars of Clay
Reading: 2 Corinthians 4:7-18

This is the age of wonders. We have seen more wonders and technological advances in the last fifty years than since the creation of the world. And yet, I believe, the greatest wonder of all is the human body.

Consider the amount of heat the body generates: 2,500 calories a day! That's enough heat to brew five pots of coffee. In spite of this, our body temperature remains constant no matter where we live or what season it is.

Our body has ten million nerve cells. Each one produces .07 volts of electricity. That is equal to 700,000 volts. Yet no one gets electrocuted. A transformer in the brain reduces the high voltage and distributes power evenly throughout the body, keeping us in good health.

Imagine how marvellous the human eyes are. There are 300,000 nerves, veins and blood vessels that lead to the eyes. It is the most perfect camera that takes colour pictures instantly, day or night. What a wonder our ears are. If you placed seventeen pianos side by side you would have 1,500 keys. That is the range of our hearing.

The heart, a piece of muscle that is as big as your fist, pumps 3,000 gallons of blood through 100,000 miles of blood vessels every day. In seventy years it beats three billion times and pumps seventy-seven billion gallons of blood. Our brain is one of God's most precious gifts. Yet we are told that even the most intelligent person in the world uses less than ten per cent of his or her brain's capacity.

Yes, the human body is a marvel. But the Bible says it is dust—and it will again be reduced to dust. It is vapour, grass, a mere flower, food for worms, temporary, corruptible, mortal.

That's not all the Bible says, though. We are told that in this mortal, perishable body, God has put a treasure, a little of His breath, a part of His spirit, a spark.

A very precious treasure, indeed—more valuable than the whole world. That is, of course, if you believe in God and in His special and precious gift of life. There are those who do not believe in God, who say that they believe in nothing.

The well-known writer Ernest Hemingway felt brave, self-sufficient and defiant when he denied the existence of God. When things did not work well for him later in life he committed suicide. When he lost his pride, he lost his desire to live.

In contrast, Joni Eareckson, who was paralyzed from the

neck down after a terrible accident, quickly discovered the hidden treasure in her broken body of clay and lives her life bringing glory to God.

Old age, illness and crises in life will not destroy us if God is in control of our lives. He has put the treasure of life in our perishable bodies.

> *We are hard pressed on every side, but not crushed; perplexed, but not in despair; persecuted, but not abandoned; struck down, but not destroyed.* (2 Corinthians 4:8-9)

Just remember: the jar may be of clay, but it contains a great treasure.

The Power of God

Reading: 1 Corinthians 1:18-31

The message of the cross is foolishness to those who are perishing, but to us who are being saved it is the power of God. (1 Corinthians 1:18)

To the person who rejects Christ and His death on the cross, the cross and its message seem simply foolish. But this "foolishness", as unbelievers see it, is precisely the power that changes lives and things. Yes, the "message of the cross" is power! The Greek word is "dunamitis"—dynamite!

Jesus on the cross is not a picture of a defeated and misguided leader. On the contrary, it is one of victory over sin and death… supernatural power in action… love. Those who thought that Jesus and His death were foolishness were later "shaking in their boots" when *"the curtain of the temple was torn in two from top to bottom.*

And the earth shook and the rocks split. And the tombs broke open and the bodies of many... were raised to life" (Matthew 27:51, 52).

This isn't only power... this is dynamite! No wonder, then, that,

> *... the centurion and his soldiers... were terrified, and exclaimed, "Surely he was the Son of God!"* (Matthew 27:54)

What is the message of the cross? It is the power that tore open the curtain of the temple that separated man from God and is still tearing down curtains and walls that separate us from God; the power that shook the earth and split the rocks and is still shaking and crumbling the rock-like hearts of men and women today; the power that broke open the tombs and raised many of the dead to life and continues to do so today when people who are spiritually or emotionally dead respond to the message of the cross.

> *God was pleased through the foolishness of what was preached to save those who believe.* (1 Corinthians 1:21)

The key here is the phrase "those who believe". But verse 22 presents a sad picture of men and women of all times: *"Jews demand miraculous signs and Greeks look for wisdom."* To unbelieving men or women, the message of the cross is foolishness until they open their hearts and eyes to the power in the message. Many are led to believe that this power should manifest itself in them through supernatural signs and miracles otherwise they have not experienced the power of God.

However, the greatest miracle that takes place when you are touched by God's power is that you are born-again. Your old broken life is exchanged for a new whole one. Despair turns into hope, darkness becomes light, death is replaced by life! Chaos becomes order and there is harmony and beauty.

Yes, the world demands miraculous signs and wonders, but there is no more powerful sign than that of the cross.

> *But we preach Christ crucified: a stumbling block to Jews and foolishness to Gentiles.* (1 Corinthians 1:22)

Which Door?
Reading: Matthew 22:1-14

Robert Murray M'Cheyne is considered one of Scotland's great Christian preachers. When he died at an early age, his had become a household name. One night he preached on Jesus' words:

> *"I am the door; whoever enters through me will be saved."* (John 10:9)

A man who had heard the sermon came to him afterward and said, "I have been a church member all my life, but I never felt close to Christ until now. When I heard you preach tonight, something clicked and I felt that Jesus was very near to me. I realized what my problem had been for all these years—I had been trying to enter through the wrong door! I had been trying to go through the door of the saints and I could not make it. But, sir, you made it clear today that I must go through the door of the sinners!"

If we are going to church week after week to prove to ourselves and strengthen our delusion that we are perfect in every way, then we are not getting any closer to Jesus because we are trying to go through the wrong door.

If we are going week after week to repeat the proud Pharisee's prayer, *"God, I thank You that I am not like other men"*

(Luke 18:11), we are not getting any closer to Jesus because we are trying to go through the wrong door.

If we go week after week and do not echo the humble prayer of the tax collector, *"God, have mercy on me, a sinner"* (Luke 18:13), we are not getting any closer to the Lord because we are trying to go through the wrong door.

There are many religions that teach that one must be purified and sinless before he or she can knock at the door. In true Christianity, one knocks at the door as a sinner so that the One who answers the door may do the healing.

Christ's door is opened to sinners, not because of their holiness and purity, but because of their sinfulness and misery. Being a sinner is our problem but knowing and acknowledging it is our hope!

Jesus said to the religious leaders:

> *"I have not come to call the righteous, but sinners to repentance."* (Luke 5:32)

The point is that Jesus calls everyone to repentance. God really loves us—weak, sinful human beings who crawl on the earth. God wants us to respond freely to His love for us. He has given us freedom to choose to either live under His rule or to do it our own way.

God wants more from us than sacrifice and religion. He wants us to turn away from the wrong door and freely enter the right door. He wants us to turn from every trace of self-centredness, pride and sin that keeps us away from Jesus.

The door is open to you now, but two things can keep you from going through: thinking you are too good or thinking you are too bad. You can never be too good or too bad to come to God. Jesus said,

> *"Ask and it will be given to you; seek and you will find; knock and the door will be opened to you."* (Matthew 7:7)

My Good Samaritan

Reading: Luke 10:25-37

A lawyer came to Jesus and asked Him a question. It was a good question, but he did not ask it because he wanted to learn. Rather, he wanted to test Jesus. He asked, "What must I do to inherit eternal life?"

Jesus, knowing the man's heart, challenged him with two other questions: "What is written in the law? How do you read it?" The lawyer correctly recited from the Ten Commandments and Jesus commended him for it—and then told him to go and put what he spoke about into practice. "Do this and you will live," He said to the lawyer.

Perhaps to gain credibility, the lawyer asked for an explanation: "But who is my neighbour?" Jesus responded by telling the story of the Good Samaritan.

Now, the usual interpretation of this parable is that we must be like the Samaritan, loving and helping our enemies. Let's look at another application of this familiar story.

The man who was robbed and left half dead represents me, you, any sinner. This man was going from Jerusalem (the city of Peace) to Jericho (the city of Curse). The road from Jerusalem to Jericho is downward, descending from 2,500 feet above sea level to about 800 feet below sea level, and seventeen miles long. It runs through rocky, desert country that, in those days, was full of robbers who would attack defenceless travellers.

This man fell among thieves. Satan is a thief (John 10:10). The thieves left him stripped and half dead. Adam and Eve in the Garden of Eden were stripped of everything but their mortal bodies. God had made them holy, complete and righteous, but

Satan stripped them from all that. He even took away their immortality, leaving them half-dead. As a result we were all born spiritually dead (Ephesians 2:1-5).

The priest and the Levite represent all empty solutions for sinners. The priest represents the condemnation of the law—no love, no pity, only judgment: "You should never have come this way. It's your own fault." The Levite represents religious instructions and ceremonies: "I can tell you the route you should have taken and the route you should take the next time."

Neither of these responses helps the poor, naked, bleeding, half-dead traveller in his need. No amount of counselling, preaching or judging would make this man better. He would have died, wounded and bleeding to death.

The human heart is in need of more than exposition, judgment and instruction. While humans are hurting and slowly dying—spiritually, emotionally and even physically—there are those who will not lift a finger to help. Yet they will glow with self-righteousness and be quick to judge.

The Good Samaritan represents Jesus, the Saviour. The Samaritans were a rejected people. Jews considered them half-breeds. Jesus, too, was rejected and despised by His own (Isaiah 53:4). Like the Samaritan, Jesus had a destination—He knew why He had come and where He was going (Luke 19:10).

The Samaritan bound up the man's wounds, getting right to the heart of the problem. Jesus' mission was to heal wounds and save people from death.

The Samaritan poured wine, a disinfectant, to wash the man's wounds. Jesus poured His blood to disinfect and wash our wounds and to give us life.

The Samaritan used oil to heal and soothe the man's wounds. Oil is a symbol of the Holy Spirit who came to soothe, heal and help us.

The Samaritan took care of the man and took him to an

inn, paying all the expenses until he would return. Jesus did all that and more. He has even promised to take us to His home to spend eternity with Him.

And the story of the Good Samaritan is not yet finished! Jesus is still looking for and finding the injured, the wounded and the dying, to help them, save them and give them eternal life with Him in heaven.

Why Wait?
Reading: Acts 22

If you want to make an easy job seem very hard, just keep putting it off. Why? Because putting off an easy thing makes it difficult, and putting off a hard one makes it almost impossible.

There are those who, no matter how busy they are and how impossible it may seem, will find time to do that extra job that has come up. Then there are those who will put off doing things even if they have nothing else to do! "I will do it later," they say or, "Yes, of course I will do it but just give me some time." These are some typical responses from people who practise procrastination.

You may have heard the saying:

> *Procrastination is my sin.*
> *It brings me nothing but sorrow.*
> *I know that I should stop it.*
> *In fact, I will—tomorrow.*

In Acts 22, when Apostle Paul gave his testimony to the commander and the crowd, he said that when Jesus appeared to him, Paul asked, "What shall I do, Lord?" and Jesus answered, "Get up, and go into Damascus. There you will be told all that you have…

to do." Paul did not procrastinate. He obeyed immediately.

A man named Ananias came to Paul after his sight was restored and said to him,

> *You will be his witness to all men of what you have seen and heard. And now what are you waiting for? Get up, be baptized and wash your sins away, calling on his name.* (Acts 22:15-16)

Why do people delay coming to Jesus and receiving His forgiveness and blessings?

Some are not yet willing to give up things that they know they will have to give up. They reason, "I will wait a little longer and then accept Jesus," not realizing or accepting that no one can guarantee them time and life.

Others just procrastinate. They put off inviting Christ into their lives and making peace with God.

Many think that because they are sinners and are bad, they can't just go to God the way they are. First they must clean up their act. And because they cannot, they wait.

And still others feel that they have not yet tried all the other ways to God, and so they wait.

You may put off buying a radio or a car, painting your house, or going back to school, because you are not sure about the colour, size or even whether you need to do it or not. But how can you put off making peace with God? How can you put off confessing your sins and asking for forgiveness from God?

If there were many ways to God, you may have had reason to wait and try them all. But there aren't many ways to God. There is only one! Jesus said:

> *"I am the way and the truth and the life. No one comes to the Father except through me."* (John 14:6)

Have you been to Jesus yet? Have you made peace with God?

Keeping the Law
Reading: Matthew 5:17-20

How many times must a law-abiding person break the law to become a law-breaker? Well, the answer is very simple: only once. And every broken law carries a consequence.

A policeman stops you for a traffic violation and you tell him that this is your first traffic violation. You try to explain that you have always been a law-abiding person, but he doesn't seem to hear you or he just ignores you and gives you a ticket anyway.

Of course, a traffic violation is not as serious as breaking God's law. Breaking the law of God—or falling short of His glory—carries the death penalty.

> *For the wages of sin is death, but the gift of God is eternal life in Christ Jesus our Lord.* (Romans 6:23)

This is true whether the sin is as "big" as murder or as "small" as gossip.

> *For whoever keeps the whole law and yet stumbles at just one point is guilty of breaking all of it.* (James 2:10)

There is only one way to escape paying the penalty, and that is through Jesus Christ who paid the price to redeem all the guilty sinners who come to Him.

How is it done? Well, first of all, you must realize that you are guilty of breaking God's law and that, no matter how hard you try, you cannot find peace and feel forgiven. The second step is to humble yourself before God, confess your sins to Him, and ask Him to forgive your sins, no matter what they were. Do this, believing that He will forgive you.

The Word of God says you can know for sure about your eternal destiny.

> *I write these things to you who believe in the name of the Son of God so that you may know that you have eternal life.* (1 John 5:13)

If you would like to be sure that you have eternal life, you may pray the following short prayer:

> *Dear Jesus, I need help. Please help me. I am a sinner and I need to put my life in order, but I know that I cannot do it alone. I have tried and failed many times. Please forgive all my sins and give me a new start. I believe that You love me and died for my sins. Come into my life and be my Lord and Saviour. I need Your peace and strength. I surrender my life and my all to You. I now believe that You have forgiven my sins and saved my soul. Thank You. Amen.*

Your Life-and-Death Decision

Reading: Acts 26

"Almost" does not count for much when the issues are about life and death. The person who jumps from one roof to another and "almost" makes it might just as well have stepped off the roof's edge to his death. The fact that he "almost" made it did not do much to save his life.

In Acts 26, the Apostle Paul boldly told King Agrippa the exciting story of his conversion and the dramatic change in his life. Paul was not ashamed to give his testimony to the king and to all those who were present.

King Agrippa's answer is a sad response to Paul's testimony:

> *You almost persuade me to become a Christian.* (Acts 26:28)

Yes, King Agrippa was almost persuaded by Paul's testimony. But the final step of faith never came. If not for his obligation to tradition, his respect for the religion of his fathers and his country, his regard to his dignity as a king and his secular interests, he might have turned to Christ immediately. Many are "almost persuaded" to be saved... but not quite.

King Agrippa's symptoms were short-sightedness, a tendency to sacrifice conviction for convenience, frequent use of such words as "later" and "almost", and a preoccupation with worldly affairs and popular approval. The only known cure for this condition is taking Jesus Christ seriously—the same Jesus that Apostle Paul proclaimed.

It was a life-and-death decision—perhaps the very same one you are wrestling with today. King Agrippa knew the cure but wasn't willing to take it. The outcome of your life does not have to be the same. Please remember that "almost" does not save anyone.

The hymn by Philip Bliss, which is translated into many languages, puts it this way:

> *"Almost persuaded," now to believe;*
> *"Almost persuaded," Christ to receive;*
> *Seems now some soul to say, "Go, Spirit, go Thy way,*
> *Some more convenient day on Thee I'll call."*
> *"Almost persuaded," come, come today;*
> *"Almost persuaded," turn not away;*
> *Jesus invites you here, angels are ling'ring near,*
> *Prayers rise from hearts so dear, O wand'rer, come.*

> "Almost persuaded," harvest is past!
> "Almost persuaded," doom comes at last!
> "Almost" cannot avail; "Almost" is but to fail!
> Sad, sad, that bitter wail, "Almost," but lost."

Dear reader, if you have never invited Jesus Christ to be your Lord and Saviour, please do it now, before it is too late.

Who Is Jesus?

Reading: John 1

"Who is Jesus that you worship Him?" people often ask. The short answer is "Jesus is God," but let me say a little more.

Jesus came to dwell with us, adding humanity to His divinity, to save us from sin. He was God-man. He was not simply a teacher, a prophet, a reformer, a rabbi, a wise man, a miracle worker or a moral teacher setting a good example. He was God in the flesh, Emmanuel—God with us.

Salvation is through Him and by Him. Jesus taught that we must come to Him, that we must follow Him. He pointed us to Himself. He told us that He is the bread of life, the light of the world, the resurrection, the way, the truth and the life. We must come to the Father by and through Him. Only God in the flesh would make those claims.

The following comments about Christ (taken from various sources) are attributed to Napoleon Bonaparte:

> "I know men, and I tell you, Jesus Christ was not a man. Superficial minds see a resemblance between Christ

and the founders of empires, and the gods of other religions. That resemblance does not exist. There is between Christianity and other religions the distance of infinity."

"In every other existence but that of Christ how many imperfections! From the first day to the last He is the same; majestic and simple; infinitely firm and infinitely gentle. He proposes to our faith a series of mysteries and commands with authority that we should believe them, giving no other reason than those tremendous words, 'I am God.'"

"Everything in Christ astonishes me. His spirit overawes me, and His will confounds me. Between Him and whoever else in the world, there is no possible term of comparison. He is truly a being by Himself. His ideas and sentiments, the truth that He announces, His manner of convincing, are not explained either by human organization or by the nature of things. His religion is a revelation from an intelligence that certainly is not that of man. One can find absolutely nowhere, but in Him alone, the imitation of the example of His life. The nearer I approach, the more carefully I examine, everything is above me—everything remains grand, of a grandeur that overpowers. I search in vain in history to find the similar to Jesus Christ or anything that can approach the gospel. Neither history, nor humanity, nor the ages, nor nature offer me anything with which I am able to compare it or to explain it. Here everything is extraordinary."

"Philosophers try to solve the mysteries of the universe by their empty dissertations. Fools: they are like the child that cries to have the moon for a plaything. Christ never hesitates. He speaks with authority, His religion is a mystery… but it subsists by its own force. He seeks, and absolutely requires, the love of men, the most difficult thing in the world to obtain. Alexander, Caesar and Hannibal conquered the world but had not friends. I myself am perhaps the only person of my day who loves Alexander, Caesar and Hannibal."

"Alexander, Caesar, Charlemagne, and myself founded empires; but upon what did we rest the creations of our genius? Upon force. Jesus Christ alone founded His empire upon love, and at this hour millions of men would die for Him. I am much struck with the contrast between Christ's mode of gathering people to Himself and the way practised by Alexander the Great, by Julius Caesar, and by myself. The people have been gathered to us by fear; they were gathered to Christ by love. Alexander, Caesar and I have been men of war, but Christ was the Prince of Peace. The people have been driven to us; they were drawn to Him. In our case there has been forced conscription; in His there was free obedience."

"I myself have inspired multitudes with such affection that they would die for me. But my presence was necessary. Now that I am in St. Helena, where are my friends? I am forgotten, soon to return to the earth, and become food for worms. What an abyss between my misery and the eternal Kingdom of Christ, who is proclaimed, loved, adored, and which is extending over all the earth. Is this death? I tell you, the death of Christ is death of a God. I tell you, JESUS CHRIST IS GOD."

Yes, Jesus is God. He can transform you and me, and our lives. Only God can give us a new life, heal us and forgive us. Because Jesus was and is God, His death on the cross was enough to pay for your sins and for mine. The question is not "Who was Jesus?" The question is "Who is Jesus?"

Do you believe Jesus is God? And if you do believe He is God, is He your Lord?

Good News of Great Importance
Reading: Luke 2:8-20, 25-38

The only news we seem to get these days is bad news. People everywhere are disappointed, discouraged and waiting for some good news. Unfortunately, it appears that major newspapers only have a couple of column inches dedicated to "good news". If that's all the good news that can be offered, this world is in bad shape.

Many people are waiting for a government or great leader to come and save them. Every time a new leader or government rises, people's hopes rise, too… only to be let down again. And so they go on waiting for a Saviour.

Things were not any different more than 2000 years ago. The world in general, and Israel in particular, was in a big mess. The only thing that could save them was a great leader, a messiah, an anointed king. The messianic hope was the only thing that kept them going.

Imagine how the shepherds felt when they saw the angel of the Lord.

> *An angel of the Lord appeared to them and the glory of the Lord shone around them, and they were terrified. But the angel said to them, "Do not be afraid. I bring you good news of great joy that will be for all the people. Today in the town of David a Saviour has been born to you; he is Christ the Lord."* (Luke 2:9-11)

Finally the Messiah had come! Their salvation was at hand! The prophet Isaiah had spoken about this day 760 years before it happened:

> *The people walking in darkness have seen a great light; on those living in the land of the shadow of death a light has dawned.* (Isaiah 9:2)

Eight days after His birth, Jesus was taken to Simeon, a man of God who was filled with the Holy Spirit. He took Jesus in his arms and praised God, saying: "O God, now I can die in peace, for my eyes have seen Your salvation!" Can you imagine what Simeon's soul felt as he held in his trembling arms the Messiah, the Christ?

There were many anointed kings, prophets and priests , but there is only one Messiah and Saviour… and His name is Jesus.

The Glory of the Lord
Reading: Luke 2:1-20

What is the first thing that comes to mind when you think of Christmas? Be honest. I wonder if we, the believers and followers of Jesus Christ, have paid enough attention to and tried to understand the birth of Jesus Christ, putting the event in its right context.

I believe that the way Christ's birth is being celebrated is an example of a terrible misunderstanding of the purpose of Christ's coming to this world. The birth, life, death and resurrection of the Son of God have been reduced to two holidays. By highlighting two "snap-shots" from His entire life, we have ended up getting a distorted and misunderstood picture of Jesus and His Mission.

The first snapshot is one of a little, beautiful-looking baby wrapped in colourful clothing in a manger with a halo over His head. There are hundreds of variations of this snapshot, depending on who the artist is. This picture is the centre of Christmas—or "Xmas"—and it is celebrated throughout December, until the 25th.

The second picture is one of a man nailed or tied to a cross between two others. This is called Easter and it comes complete with all kinds of celebrations and trappings.

However, these two events, when taken out of context, obscure and distort God and His mission for mankind. For the beauty of Christmas is not the little child in the manger with a bright halo over His head. Rather, it is the love of God, who loved us to the point of coming to this world in the person of Jesus to save mankind, which we must be thankful for.

His glory was not found in a halo but, rather, all around Him.

The heavens declare the glory of God; the skies proclaim the work of his hands. (Psalm 19:1)

I believe, though, that only those whose spiritual eyes have been opened can see the glory and majesty of God (see Acts 7:55).

The first people to be informed of this unique birth were not the religious leaders in Jerusalem but shepherds on the Judean hillside. These were humble men who were faithful and ready to hear God's message.

No matter how ordinary or humble your place of work and duty may be, it is your place of vision if you keep your eyes open and your ears tuned to God's glory.

Without a deeper understanding of Christ and His love toward us, Christmas is just a religious festival with no real meaning. What we should be celebrating is God's visit to our planet in the person of Jesus Christ. His visit began in a manger and took Him to the cross and, along the way, had nowhere to lay His head.

The shepherds had seen the glory of the Lord. They had met their "Christ", the Messiah. They would never be the same.

> *And we, who with unveiled faces all reflect the Lord's glory, are being transformed into his likeness with ever-increasing glory, which comes from the Lord, who is the Spirit.* (2 Corinthians 3:18)

Immanuel

Reading: Isaiah 9:2-7

If you had a very important message to bring to the entire human race, how would you do it? Would you use a loud, booming voice from heaven? Would you broadcast it on every television channel at once? Or would you write the message across the sky?

Well, I don't know how you would do it, but I know how God did it. He sent His important message through a person—delivered in a manger, nailed to a cross and then raised up from the grave. In fact, Jesus is God's message.

> *In the beginning was the Word, and the Word was with God, and the Word was God.... The Word became flesh and made his dwelling among us. We have seen his glory, the glory of the One and Only, who came from the Father, full of grace and truth.* (John 1:1,14)

Christ was before Bethlehem. He said in John 8:58, *"Before Abraham was born, I AM!"* Jesus appears in the first verse of the

Bible and remains throughout the Old Testament until His appearance in the flesh.

"*He became flesh*" is the key to understanding the true meaning of Christmas. The prophet Isaiah, 760 years before Christ's birth in Bethlehem, made a very clear distinction when he said, "*For to us a child is born, to us a son is given*" (Isaiah 9:6). A child was *born*, but a Son was *given*.

God takes Isaiah into the future and shows him the people of the world who, for a long time, walked in darkness and in the shadow of death. Suddenly they see a great light, a light that will set them free and break their chains of bondage, both physical and spiritual.

> *The people walking in darkness have seen a great light; on those living in the land of the shadow of death a light has dawned.... For to us a child is born, to us a son is given, and the government will be on his shoulders. And he will be called Wonderful Counsellor, Mighty God, Everlasting Father, Prince of Peace.* (Isaiah 9:2,6)

In Matthew 1:23 we have a direct quote from Isaiah 7:14. "*The virgin will be with child and will give birth to a son, and they will call him Immanuel, which means 'God with us.'*" Here, the name Immanuel is clearly describing the divinity of Christ. But let's look at four other names given to the child in Bethlehem.

WONDERFUL COUNSELLOR—in Hebrew, "Pele Yoetz". Christ is not our prosecutor, but our counsellor and defender.

MIGHTY GOD—in Hebrew, "El Gibbor". Jesus is given the name of God!

EVERLASTING FATHER—in Hebrew, "Abhi Ad" which is literally translated as "Father of Eternity".

Prince of Peace—in Hebrew, "Sar Shalom". Shalom means more than the peace obtained from the absence of war. It includes prosperity, well-being, harmony, peace in one's heart and peace with God. It is the perfect state of being.

God, in the person of His Son, came to this world in the flesh as a poor humble child to save the world and bring peace. Have you found the Prince of Peace yet? If you have, rejoice and celebrate for you have found real and eternal life.

Coffee Break

What Will You Give?

"What can I give to our King?" you ask sadly.
"I have nothing worthwhile to bring," you say with tears.
"I have nothing that the Lord Jesus would want," you whisper
in disappointment.

Oh, but listen, dear friend!
We all have gifts that we may bring,
We all have songs that we may sing,
We all have words that we may say,
We all have prayers that we may pray,
We all have love and joy that we may give.

And what a joy life is when we scatter about
The things God has given us to share.

So, dear friend,
If you want to give a gift, give it!
If it is a song, sing it!
If it is a talent, use it!
If it is love, spread it!
If you have religion, live it!
If you have gladness, share it!
If you have a prayer, pray it!

"Behold! I Stand at the Door and Knock!"

Reading: Revelation 3:14-22

"Behold! I stand at the door and knock!" This was the message sent to the believers in Laodicea. They claimed to be rich and independent, but they did not realize that they had drifted away from God and become worldly. They were neither totally with God, nor totally with the world.

God is not pleased with indecisive people. People that are neither here nor there are good for no one. God compares them to lukewarm water:

> *"So, because you are lukewarm—neither hot nor cold—I am about to spit you out of my mouth."* (Revelation 3:16)

Why was Jesus so harsh with them? Because He loved them!

> *"Those whom I love I rebuke and discipline. So be earnest, and repent."* (Revelation 3:19)

Revelation 3:20 shows us four great things:

1) GOD TAKES THE FIRST STEP.

   He is calling you. Do you sense Him knocking?

2) A DOOR STANDS BETWEEN YOU AND GOD.

   It could be something wrong—a habit, a relationship, a resentment—or something good that is too important to you.

3) God Does Not Force Himself in.

"*If anyone hears my voice and opens the door....*" He knocks and speaks, but *you* must open the door. Faith is opening the door and asking Jesus to come into your life.

4) Jesus Wants to Share in Our Every Day Life.

"*I will go in and eat with him....*" He wants to be there when you work and play, in your good times and bad times, during your ups and downs.

There are three responses to Christ knocking on our hearts' doors: to many Christ is a stranger on the outside, to some He is only a guest and is given a room, and to others He is Master and Lord.

That door with the doorknob only on the inside makes all the difference. Where is Christ today? Is He in your life or standing outside and knocking to come in?

Metamorphosis
Reading: Colossians 4:1-17

Several years ago, in the summer, I was on my balcony when I found a beautiful moth. It was large and colourful enough to be mistaken for a butterfly. I decided to read and learn about moths and butterflies.

I was fascinated by the life cycles of these winged creatures—from egg to caterpillar to pupa to a moth that spreads its wings and flies away. This entire process of changes is called metamorphosis (changing of appearance).

This process is a picture of the transformation that takes place in a person when he or she is born-again. Before we come to Christ for His changing touch, we are like caterpillars—earthbound and helpless—hoping that we will get through life without being stepped on and squashed to death. For all intents and purposes, we are already spiritually dead.

> *As for you, you were dead in your transgressions and sins, in which you used to live when you followed the ways of this world.... But... God... made us alive with Christ even when we were dead in transgressions.* (Ephesians 2:1-2,4,5)

Just as the caterpillar must become a pupa and die as a caterpillar before it becomes a "new creature" that can fly, we also must go through the process of transformation. The old nature, the cocoon of sin, has to die before we are liberated and a new life is created.

> *For we know that our old self was crucified with him so that the body of sin might be done away with, that we should no longer be slaves to sin—because anyone who has died has been freed from sin.* (Romans 6:6-7)

That is what the "new life" is all about. A true believer is no longer a caterpillar stuck to the ground—a true believer is a butterfly who can fly and live above the ground! That is why Paul writes to the believers:

> *Since, then, you have been raised with Christ, set your hearts on things above, where Christ is seated at the right hand of God. Set your minds on things above, not on earthly things.* (Colossians 3:1-2)

If you are serious about living this new life with Christ, act like it. Live your new life. Your old life is dead. Your new life—your real life—is with Christ in God. Reject and remove everything that is connected with the old way of death. Whatever you did in the past, you did because you did not know any better. But you know better now, so you must make sure that all the bad is gone forever. Your old clothes are burned in the fire and you are now dressed in a brand new wardrobe.

God has made you a prince or a princess. Act like one; live like one! Just as a butterfly no longer crawls like a caterpillar, nor desires to do so, so it is with a born-again Christian who is given a new life. He or she does not want to go back into the old deadly way of life in search of joy and happiness. He or she is now connected directly to the manufacturer of joy, peace and life: God Himself.

Live your new life in Him and enjoy it!

Emptiness
Reading: John 4:1-42

In today's corrupt and selfish society, you will find many people asking, "What is happiness? What is real joy?" Several years ago, there was a young lady who would call me with similar questions. She was searching for peace, joy and some meaning and happiness in life.

One day she called me and said that there was no joy in her heart. I asked her, "What *do* you feel, then, in your heart?" She quickly responded, "Nothing. I feel nothing." When I questioned how one could feel "nothing", she repeated her answer: "Nothing. I feel nothing in there. I am empty."

Unfortunately, she was not an isolated case. Even King Solomon, who had everything a person could ever want—riches, fame, pleasures—wrote:

> *"Meaningless! Meaningless!" says the Teacher, "Utterly meaningless! Everything is meaningless." What does man gain from all his labor at which he toils under the sun? .... All things are wearisome, more than one can say. The eye has never enough of seeing, nor the ear its fill of hearing.... I have seen all the things that are done under the sun; all of them are meaningless, a chasing after the wind.* (Ecclesiastes 1:2-3,8,14)

We read in the Bible about someone else who was seeking satisfaction in life. In John 4:1-42, we see a Samaritan woman who had tried everything in life but was still empty. The Bible says that she had been married five times and that, although she was currently living with a man, she still had no peace or joy. She wanted joy that was lasting—her repeatedly failed relationships had been temporary pleasures that led her nowhere.

Jesus told her about Living Water. He pointed out that the things of the world would never satisfy and that people without Christ would always be thirsty. She asked for the Living Water that Jesus offered her, thinking that it was literally physical water.

Suddenly she found herself confronted by her sins. Jesus told her to go call her husband, knowing that she was not married to the man she was living with. He wanted to convict her of her sins and to have her confess them. No one who hides his or her sin can be saved.

The woman immediately tried to change the topic of conversation. Many who are convicted of sin today try to change the subject by arguing about differences in religion. "Where should we worship?" and "Which religion is right?" are some typical questions.

Worldly pleasures, and even religion, cannot satisfy spiritual thirst. Only the Living Water that comes from Christ—eternal life—can satisfy and fill the emptiness in our hearts.

Sadhu Sundar Singh, an Indian evangelist whom my father greatly admired, once said:

> "I was dying of thirst. When my spiritual eyes were opened, I saw rivers of living water flowing from his pierced side. I drank of it and was satisfied. Thirst was no more. Ever since, I have always drunk of that water of life, and have never been athirst in the sandy desert of this world."

What Are You Searching for?

Reading: Romans 3:22-26

In a popular tabloid, Elizabeth Taylor was once quoted as saying, "God knows I have tried: I have tried fame, food, men, drugs and drink, but I have never found peace." The story continues, stating that as Taylor looked at her sleeping mother so very near death, she said sadly, "Maybe death is the only peace."

A reporter asked Elvis Presley, six weeks before he died, "Elvis, when you started playing music, you said you wanted three things in life: you wanted to be rich, you wanted to be famous and you wanted to be happy. Are you happy, Elvis?" Presley replied, "No, I am as lonely as hell."

It seems that riches, fame, so-called friends, and even youth and health do not necessarily bring peace and happiness. Elizabeth Taylor and Elvis Presley had all of the above, except for peace and happiness!

And they are not the exception. The world is full of rich and famous people that are miserable and lonely. The number of people committing suicide, most of them young, in the prime of their lives, is ever increasing. Loneliness and depression are the most frequently diagnosed problems. The poor and the sick are not the only ones affected by loneliness, fear, depression and anxiety. Men and women, the rich and the poor, the young and the old everywhere are yearning to find some happiness and peace. Unfortunately, few find it.

Why? Why can't we find peace and happiness? What is the problem? The problem is our separation from God. The Bible confirms this separation:

> *Remember that at that time you were separate from Christ... without hope and without God in the world.* (Ephesians 2:12)

This problem of separation affects all mankind because,

> *... all have sinned and fall short of the glory of God.* (Romans 3:23)

We are, by nature, sinful creatures standing apart from a Holy God. This sin problem leaves all of us with an emptiness that must be filled.

Pascal, the great mathematician once said, "In each of us there is a God-shaped vacuum yearning to be filled."

How do we overcome this sin barrier? The solution to the problem must come from God's side, for each of us has already sinned. God's solution is Jesus Christ, who is the *"Prince of Peace"* (Isaiah 9:6). The Hebrew word used is "Sar Shalom" and has a much wider meaning than the term "peace". It does not only mean absence of war and strife, but it includes prosperity, well-being, harmony within and without, peace in one's heart and peace with God. It is the perfect state of man.

We read about God's solution in His Holy Word:

"For God so loved the world that He gave His one and only Son, that whoever believes in Him shall not perish but have eternal life." (John 3:16)

God did His part to reach you. He wants you to have peace, joy and eternal life. Do you have peace and joy? Or have doubts and fears become a way of life for you?

If you are searching for happiness, joy and peace, you will only find it in Jesus Christ who died for each one of us. He wants you to have lasting peace and eternal life. You can make peace with God right now by asking Him to come into your heart and life. You can do that by praying a simple prayer like this:

Dear Jesus, I need help. Please help me. I am a sinner and need to put my life in order but I know I can't do it alone. I have tried and failed many times. Please forgive all my sins and give me a new start. I believe that You love me and died for my sins. Come into my life and be my Lord and Saviour. I need Your peace and strength. I surrender my life and my all to You. I now believe that You have forgiven my sins and saved my soul. Thank You.

Coffee Break

Stop Searching

(To the tune of an old Armenian-Turkish hymn)

*Stop searching, O my soul,
Throughout this world of ours;
There's no peace for us down here,
But only loneliness.*

*Your friends and family,
Sadly, cannot give you that
Which they, too, are searching for;
And so you're left alone.*

*Even riches and power
Are powerless to fill
The emptiness that is in you
And give you happiness.*

*Man-made religions, too,
Cannot satisfy you;
But only Christ who died for you
Can fully satisfy you.*

*Stop searching, O my soul,
Before it is too late,
And turn to Christ, your Creator,
And live forevermore.*

Guilty!

Reading: Romans 8

You have failed someone who was counting on you. Guilt is written all over your face. You have lost your joy and you can't even read the Bible or pray without feeling guilt and shame.

GUILTY! You are guilty. Even if people don't say it to your face, you know or you feel that they are saying it to others or are judging you in their hearts. And there is nothing you can do about what they say or think.

GUILTY! That's the unspoken verdict for many individuals who have faced failure in their life but, as the Apostle Peter discovered, God's forgiveness is as near as a prayer.

> *Then Peter remembered the word Jesus had spoken: "Before the rooster crows, you will disown me three times." And he went outside and wept bitterly.* (Matthew 26:75)

Have you ever felt like Peter... guilty, discouraged and ashamed, not knowing what else you could do? You lower your head in shame and remorse and cry out: "Please, God, have mercy on me!"

Oh, dear reader, I know those feelings. I have been there. Let me remind you that when you can no longer lift your guilty eyes to God, you can be sure that God is still looking at you... not with the angry expression of an irritated parent, but rather with compassion, love and tenderness.

And when you don't even expect Him to forgive you, He reaches out in grace and love—and reminds you that you are

His own and He cares for you. He wipes away your tears of remorse and He encourages you to try again. If your eyes are clouded with tears of guilt and failure today, run to your heavenly Father's arms. He is ready to turn your weeping into tears of joy.

Just remember:

> *"So if the Son sets you free, you will be free indeed."* (John 8:36)

and...

> *Therefore, there is now no condemnation for those who are in Christ Jesus.* (Romans 8:1)

Caught in the Act!
Reading: John 8:1-12

The religious leaders were anxious to trick and trap Jesus into saying something wrong so that they would have a charge against Him. They would ask questions about His authority, about the Sabbath, about His claims, etc.

This time they wanted to bring about a conflict between Jesus and Moses. Moses had said, *"If a man commits adultery... both the adulterer and the adulteress must be put to death"* (Leviticus 20:10). So the religious leaders *"brought in a woman caught in the act of adultery. And they made her stand in the middle of the crowd,"* probably facing Jesus.

Obviously, this incident was staged to trap Jesus. The religious leaders wanted Jesus to contradict the Law of Moses so that they could then turn the people against Jesus. They reminded Jesus of Moses' command that adulterers be stoned to death. Would Jesus agree with this penalty?

On examination of this case, we see that the woman was guilty and did not plead innocence, nor did Jesus charge her accusers with lying.

What did Jesus do? John 8:6 says, *"But Jesus bent down and started to write on the ground with his finger."* The Bible doesn't tell us what Jesus wrote. He may have written the commandment in Leviticus 20:10 to remind the people that both guilty parties were to be stoned... not only one of them. (The man who committed adultery with the woman had not been brought to Jesus!)

Whatever Jesus had written, the leaders were clearly dissatisfied with His silence and insisted He respond. Jesus looked around for a sinless accuser and found none. He was telling the people that, yes, the law had to be carried out, but it was to be done by those who had committed no sins.

In this way, Jesus upheld the Law of Moses. He did not excuse the woman's sin or say that she was not guilty, deserving the penalty. What He did do is accuse every one of those men of having sinned also.

Those who wish to judge others should be pure themselves. This doesn't mean that we are free to sin just because everyone else does. We are guilty of sin even if we aren't caught in the act of sinning.

After Jesus wrote on the ground a second time, the accusers began to walk away, each one aware of his own sins. As Jesus pointed out to the woman, no one was left to condemn her. She then heard these comforting words from Jesus—words full of grace and truth:

> *"Neither do I condemn you.... Go now and leave your life of sin."* (John 8:11)

Jesus did not approve of her sin, but He did forgive her for it. Whether you feel like one of the accusers or the accused, come to Jesus. He will forgive you no matter what you have done.

Jesus Anointed by a Sinner
Reading: Luke 7:36-50

When a woman who had lived a sinful life in that town learned that Jesus was eating at the Pharisee's house, she brought an alabaster jar of perfume, and as she stood behind Him at His feet weeping, she began to wet His feet with her tears. Then she wiped them with her hair, kissed them and poured perfume on them. (Luke 7:37-38)

The extent of this woman's worship and sacrifice revealed her conviction that Jesus was worthy of her worship and that there was nothing too good for Him.

Simon's attitude was quite different. He did not like the idea at all. Here she was a sinner, a prostitute in his house, and Jesus, instead of asking her to go away, allowed her to wash His feet and touch Him. Simon could not understand it at all.

However, Jesus knew why this woman had come to do this, and why Simon was objecting. Jesus knew that this woman had heard Jesus preach and, in repentance, she had decided to live a new life. She came to Jesus out of love and with the understanding that she could be forgiven. She wanted to start a new life and she believed that Jesus would forgive her sins.

The alabaster jar with the costly perfume was probably the most valuable thing she had, and she offered it to Jesus. Jesus accepted her offering and publicly announced to the woman that her sins had been forgiven.

Jesus saw two things here: the love and devotion of the woman, who gave her heart to be Jesus' home, and the hypocrisy and neglect of Simon, who had given Him a very cool welcome, not even extending the usual courtesies of washing his guest's feet, kissing His cheek and giving Him oil for His head.

Dear reader, how will you welcome Jesus? Will you make your heart Christ's home?

Unconfessed Sin

Reading: Psalm 32

Many Christians have lost their joy and live miserable, weakened and often sickly lives because of unconfessed sin. They either don't think that God will forgive them, or they are too proud to confess their sins to God and ask for forgiveness. But unconfessed sins and guilt are worse and deadlier than a physical disease. Sin destroys the body and the spirit.

This is a major problem among many Christians today—Christians who have been living defeated lives. A person with this particular problem can become well if he deals with his sin and guilt, just as King David did.

His prayer went like this:

> *Be merciful to me, O LORD, for I am in distress; my eyes grow weak with sorrow, my soul and my body with grief. My life is consumed by anguish and my years by groaning; my strength fails because of my affliction, and my bones grow weak.* (Psalm 31:9-10)

When David confessed his sins and asked for forgiveness, he saw and felt the healing that took place in his life. And now he shares this wonderful experience with others:

> *Blessed is he whose transgressions are forgiven, whose sins are covered.... When I kept silent, my bones wasted away through my groaning all day long. For day and night your hand was heavy upon me; my strength was sapped as in the heat of summer. Then I acknowledged my sin to you and did not cover up my iniquity. I said, "I will confess my transgressions to the LORD"—and you forgave the guilt of my sin.* (Psalm 32:1,3-5)

God is still healing and mending the lives of those who come to Him. How is your spiritual health? Have you dealt with your unconfessed sins yet? Your spiritual and physical health depends on it! If you have not, please do it now, so you can start to live again. The Holy Spirit will help you do it.

True Repentance

Reading: Joel 2:12-32

"It's too late now, too late to be sorry for what you have done. You should have thought of the consequences before you did what you did! Now it's too late." A father may say this to his son, or a wife to her husband, or a husband to his wife. "How can I ever forgive you for what you have done?"

Has anyone ever told you it was too late to be forgiven, even though you pleaded for forgiveness? It is an awful thing to be told that you will never be forgiven.

Even though Judah was unfaithful to God and, as a result,

was devastated by a terrible locust plague and severe drought, God did not tell Judah, "It's too late now" or "We'll see." Rather, God spoke through the prophet Joel and said:

> *Even now, declares the Lord, return to me with all your heart, with fasting and weeping and mourning. Rend your heart and not your garments. Return to the Lord your God, for he is gracious and compassionate, slow to anger and abounding in love, and he relents from sending calamity.* (Joel 2:12-13)

Then a general invitation was extended to everyone:

> *And everyone who calls on the name of the Lord will be saved….* (Joel 2:32)

"Everyone who calls on the name of the Lord" does not mean an occasional call or claiming to be a Christian or even faithfully participating in Christian activities and services. Empty words and promises do not impress God.

God spoke through Joel and said: *"Rend your hearts and not your garments."* Charles Spurgeon, in one of his sermons, said:

> *Garment rending and other outward signs of religious emotion are easily manifested and are frequently hypocritical; but to feel true repentance is far more difficult, and consequently far less common. Men will attend to the most multiplied and minute ceremonial regulations; for such things are pleasing to the flesh, but true religion is too humbling, too heart searching, too thorough for the tastes of the carnal men; they prefer something more ostentatious, flimsy and worldly. Outward observances are temporarily comfortable; eye and ear are pleased; self-conceit is fed, and self-righteousness is puffed up: but they are ultimately delusive, for in the time of death*

> *and at the day of judgment, the soul needs something more substantial than ceremonies and rituals to lean upon. Apart from vital godliness all religion is utterly vain; offered without a sincere heart, every form of worship is a solemn sham and an impudent mockery of the majesty of heaven.*

Garment rending, or whatever other outward expression or sign, may give a person some spiritual satisfaction, ease the conscience and may impress others... but not God! God wants to see the rending of the heart, not superficial acts that exclude the heart. Unless the heart is involved in the act of repentance, there can be no real repentance and, where there is no real repentance, there can be no forgiveness and justification. What pleases God more than outward acts of religion is a broken and contrite heart.

When David was convicted of sin, he cried out to God and said:

> *Have mercy on me, O God.... Wash away all my iniquity and cleanse me from my sin.... my sin is always before me. Against you, you only, have I sinned and done what is evil in your sight.... Save me... O God.... You do not delight in sacrifice or I would bring it; you do not take pleasure in burnt offerings. The sacrifices of God are broken spirit; a broken and contrite heart, O God, you will not despise.* (Psalm 51:1-4,14,16-17)

God's divine appeal to Judah to repent is still being made today to every human being. Even now, the Lord calls people to repentance. It is not too late to return to Him. But it must be more than an outward ritual.

God wanted the people of Judah to turn to Him with their

hearts, with fasting, with weeping and with mourning. Why should it be different with us, and why should God expect less from us? Are we not all sinners in desperate need of salvation?

Our hearts are as hard as stone, but Jesus who died on the cross for our sins is ready to replace our corrupt hearts and give us new ones.

> *I will give you a new heart and put a new spirit in you; I will remove from you your heart of stone and give you a heart of flesh. And I will put my Spirit in you and move you to follow my decrees and be careful to keep my laws.* (Ezekiel 36:26-27)

May God help us to hear the voice of the Holy Spirit who is convicting us of sin, to humble ourselves and pray, to seek God's face and to turn away from our wicked ways. Let us rend our hearts, not garments. Then, and only then, will God forgive our sins and give us a new heart and eternal life!

Forgiveness

Reading: Matthew 18:21-35

If love is the essence of Christianity and sets it apart from all other religions (as stated in 1 Corinthians 13), then forgiveness—or forgiving love—is the essence of God's salvation. If not for God's willingness to forgive our sins and bring peace into our lives, there would be no way out for us. It is His love, coupled with His forgiveness, that brings meaning and peace in the lives of the true believers.

When asked, *"Lord, how many times shall I forgive?"* Jesus responded with a fascinating story. He compared the Kingdom of Heaven to an earthly king who wanted to settle accounts with his servants. Three things stand out in this story, each one difficult—if not impossible—to count or measure.

Our Debt to God

Our debt to God is compared with the debt of the servant who owed 10,000 talents. According to Bible commentaries, this amount is somewhere between six and twelve million dollars. The original Greek uses the word "myriad"—which implies that the amount cannot be calculated or measured.

Jesus makes it clear that our debt to God cannot be counted. As far as God is concerned, we are bankrupt!

God's Love for Us

The debt had to be paid, but this man *"was not able to pay."* The only option left was for him and all his belongings to be sold. However, the king was a compassionate man.

The servant in debt did two things. First, he admitted that he had nothing with which to pay his debts and then he begged for his master's pity and mercy. Verse 27 says that *"the servant's master took pity on him, cancelled the debt and let him go."* Thus, the master himself paid the debt. He did this, not because the servant was bankrupt, but *"because you begged me to."*

We all are destitute, spiritually bankrupt—and we must ask to be forgiven because we have nothing to offer God toward the payment of our debt of sin. All our good deeds, money, religion, etc., are not enough.

Just like the king in this story, God our heavenly King paid our debt by sending His Son Jesus to die on the cross to pay the price of our salvation. All that is left for us to do is humbly accept His sacrifice for us. Then we must serve Him—not to pay back our debt, but because the debt is paid.

Our Forgiveness of Others

The Jewish tradition taught that when a person wronged you, you should forgive three times. Peter suggested seven times. But Jesus said *"seventy times seven"*, implying that we should lose count of how often we forgive someone. Think of how often God has forgiven you. We must be willing to forgive others if we expect forgiveness from God.

Additional reading: Matthew 6:12, 14-15; 18:35

The Joy of Forgiveness
Reading: Psalm 32

King David's life was one of success and glory... until he became careless and lazy, giving in to temptation and committing adultery and murder. He even deceitfully covered the whole matter for a year. Then God spoke to him through a prophet named Nathan and David finally confessed his sins.

David begins Psalm 32 by acknowledging God's forgiveness. Then we see three stages David went through.

The Pain of Unconfessed Sin

What happened to David when he refused to admit and confess his sins? He suffered spiritually and physically. He became like an old man and completely dried up!

Many people who are suffering from similar symptoms (i.e. anxiety, fears, mental fatigue, etc.) are going to doctors when their problems can often be traced back to unconfessed sin. The only doctor who can cure that kind of pain is God.

The Cry of Confession

David immediately confessed that he had sinned. His prayer was not a general confession. He named his sins specifically and God, being faithful to His word, forgave him.

> *Who is a God like you, who pardons sin and forgives the transgression of the remnant of his inheritance? You do not stay angry forever but delight to show mercy.* (Micah 7:18)

> *If we confess our sins, he is faithful and just and will forgive us our sins and purify us from all unrighteousness.* (1 John 1:9)

The Joy of Forgiveness

David's sighing was replaced with singing. He was surrounded by songs of joy. Wherever he turned, he discovered something to sing about. It used to be that wherever he turned, he saw his sins. David was no longer afraid because God was his hiding place.

Remember that being forgiven and cleansed does not guarantee perfection and smooth sailing. Satan tries hard to undermine and ruin the peace and confidence of the believer. The believer begins to worry about his past sins and their results.

There are bitter fruits from disobedience, as David found out. But verses 10 and 11 assure us that God protects and upholds those who belong to Him. The wicked have many sorrows, but the cleansed and forgiven believer enjoys the loving kindness and mercy of God.

Coffee Break

A New Year—A New Page

She approached me with tears in her eyes and with trembling lips.
Her homework is done, I thought, but why is she crying?
"Dad, I want a new paper, please," she said,
"I have spoiled this one. I am sorry."
I took the paper in my hands and looked.
It was stained and wrinkled.
"You should have been careful," I said.
And then I gave her a new one, unspotted and clean.
Looking into her sad eyes, I smiled,
"Do better now. Be careful, my child."

I approached the great throne with trembling soul.
The old year is gone.
"Heavenly Father, do You have a new page for me?
I have spoiled and wasted this one."
With tears in my eyes and trembling heart full of
guilt and shame, I just stood there.
He stretched His hand and took my old page,
wrinkled and stained,
And gave me a new one, unspotted and clean.
Then He smiled and with a voice sweeter
than any I had ever heard, He said to me,
"Do better now. Be careful, my child."
And then He wiped away the tears from my eyes.

One More Year

Reading: Luke 13:1-9

The end of one year is the beginning of another and, for most people, a time to take an inventory of our lives. It is time to remember our failures, learn from them and then forget them again. As Paul said,

> *Forgetting what is behind and straining toward what is ahead, I press on toward the goal....* (Philippians 3:13-14)

When we consider our failures, we must be honest and deliberate. In particular, we must look at our fruitfulness for the Lord.

In the parable of the fig tree, there are three things to keep in mind. First of all, we must apply the parable to our Christian lives in retrospect. The owner of the vineyard is God the Father, the gardener is our Lord Jesus Christ and the fruit-bearing plants are we, the Christians.

Have we borne fruit for our Lord in the springtime of our lives? Or did we misuse those golden months of our youth? Did we bear fruit as young adults, giving God the first and best of our strength or did we allow sin to consume the strength of our early manhood and womanhood?

As middle-aged adults do we still allow our years to be eaten up by worldliness? Are we a half-century old by the calendar but still spiritual babies? These are questions we need to ask ourselves—and answer honestly—as we consider our lives in retrospect.

Secondly, we must note the words of Jesus as He intercedes on our behalf with God the Father: *"Lord... leave it alone for one more year. I'll dig around it and fertilize it."*

Do you see the Lord's great mercy here? How often has He given us a second chance? We must view this year as a grant from God's infinite grace. Time belongs to God and only His mercy holds back the axe of justice. Shall we insult God's mercy by giving Him less than our best in the coming year?

Thirdly, there is an implication of the limit of God's grace and patience. The gardener asked for a reprieve of no longer than one year. Even when Jesus is the pleader, the request of mercy has its limits.

Let us ask ourselves if this year is our last and if we are prepared to hear the midnight cry, *"Here is the bridegroom!"*

Some of us had friends and family members for whom this was their last year. This parable should really shake any Christian who is giving less than his or her best to the Lord. Now is the time to obey the commands of our Lord, for we have no assurance of tomorrow.

> *Do not boast about tomorrow, for you do not know what a day may bring forth.* (Proverbs 27:1)

As Jesus, our gardener, cultivates and fertilizes us with the Holy Word of God, let us each resolve to bear fruit for Him during the year.

Healing

Reading: James 5:13-20

"*H*ealth is the most important thing," people say. What good is money, beauty or education to a person who is sick and suffering? Many of our tax dollars go toward Medicare. People are preoccupied with their health—or lack of it. Diets, exercise machines and videos are being marketed with the promise that they will improve and prolong our lives.

Many sicknesses are the result of birth defects or accidents. We all are subject to the natural laws and we will get sick from time to time. However, there are sicknesses that are caused by an individual's attitude and lifestyle—sicknesses that can been prevented. Problems such as overeating, drug addiction, smoking, alcoholism and even uncleanness usually lead to illness and deterioration of the body. Emotions such as tension, fear, sorrow, envy, resentment and hatred can also lead to sickness.

The concept of healing in the Bible means much more than being cured from an illness. It means "wholeness of body and spirit." Let us look at three approaches to healing found in the Bible.

God's Miraculous Intervention

...according to His sovereign will and purpose. The Bible is full of examples and even today there is plenty of evidence of miraculous healings everywhere. Yet God does not heal all those who call on Him or who are prayed for by others. Apostle Peter assures us that *"God does not show favoritism"* (Acts 10:34).

But God *does* heal some people and not others. Why? Because… *"His ways are higher than our ways"* (Isaiah 55:8).

This shouldn't discourage us from praying for the sick, though. Jesus said to *"pray without ceasing"* (Luke 18:1).

The New Birth

When a person becomes a "new creature" in Christ, he or she becomes a new person. It is the testimony of many that when they made a commitment to follow Christ, made things right spiritually and began to live a godly life, many of their illnesses were taken away.

The new birth brings a new life and attitude with it. Many things that made us sick before are no longer with us.

THE CONFESSION OF SIN

Many Christians live miserable, weakened and often sickly lives because of disobedience and unconfessed sins. Unconfessed sins and guilt are worse than a physical disease. Sin destroys the body and the spirit.

King David is a good example (Psalm 31:9-10). When David confessed his sin, he felt healing take place in his life.

> *When I kept silent, my bones wasted away through my groaning all day long. Then I acknowledged my sin to you and did not cover up my iniquity. I said, "I will confess my transgressions to the Lord"—and you forgave the guilt of my sin.* (Psalm 32:3,5)

God still heals the lives of those who go to Him.

Who Can Solve Our Problems?

Reading: Matthew 9:1-8,18-38

A few years ago, my wife was talking to me about some conversations she had had with people she knew well and others whom she hardly knew. She was speaking to me passionately and I could see pain on her face. When I interrupted her with a comment, she stopped for a moment and then exclaimed, "Everyone has a problem! What's going on? There is so much pain out there."

Yes, there are problems, no matter where you look. Babies have problems; children and young people have problems; parents, husbands and wives; governments and politicians; churches, their members and leaders; you and I… we all have problems!

There are all kinds of problems... and there are many of them. But the biggest problem is that there are few, if any, problem solvers. It wouldn't matter how big your problem was if you knew an infinite Problem Solver.

Sickness, guilt, financial uncertainty, loss of a loved one, doubts, fears, loneliness and depression are only some of the problems people have to deal with on a daily basis. And people will try almost anything to solve their problems... anything except the right thing.

What is the right thing? Of course, the right thing is to go to the Master Problem Solver—Jesus, God Himself!

But that is too simple and unrealistic for some people, and so they go on searching for someone or something else to fix their problems... all in vain.

In Matthew 9, we see that Jesus has both the ability and the authority to solve problems—physical, emotional and spiritual. The problem, of course, was that people were not willing to accept Jesus. Some were indifferent to His claims, others were angry. But those who believed Him and accepted His claims and came to Him had their needs met and their problems solved.

To the questioning and rebellious heart, Jesus proved His authority to forgive sins by demonstrating His power to heal. The effect was instantaneous and remarkable: the people feared and glorified God (verse 8). Then, one after the other, a paralyzed man, a ruler, a woman who was bleeding for twelve years, two blind men and a mute demoniac crossed His path.

Jesus met their personal needs with strong but tender words and spoke to each one of them a message of peace and courage. Jesus continued His ministry... preaching, teaching, healing and spreading the Good News of the Kingdom. And He still does today.

Dear friend, God may not always give you the wisdom to

solve your own problem, but you can be sure that Jesus is strong enough to handle it, compassionate enough to feel it, loving enough to care for it and wise enough to deal with it. Turn your worries over to the One who never fails to solve our problems.

Is Death the End?

Reading: 1 Thessalonians 4

If you have ever been to a funeral home or service, or been in the company of mourners, you will understand what Paul wrote in 1 Thessalonians 4:13-18. Of course, Christians are expected to feel sorrow and shed tears when a loved one dies, but we are not to sorrow like people of the world who have no hope. Even Jesus cried when Lazarus, one of His best friends, died (John 11:32-36). We all must go through the valley of the shadow of death. But in the midst of our sorrow, there must be the assurance of the living hope we have in Christ.

> *Praise be to the God and Father of our Lord Jesus Christ! In his great mercy he has given us new birth into a living hope through the resurrection of Jesus Christ from the dead.* (1 Peter 1:3)

Sorrow had come to the lives of the Thessalonian believers and they were wondering whether their dead Christian loved ones would be left behind at the return of Christ. Paul assured them that the dead will be raised first, and then all those believers who are alive will join them.

Note the three comforting assurances that believers have in times of sorrow:

Death for the Believer Is Sleep

"Sleep in Jesus" means "put to sleep through Jesus." Of course, the soul goes to be with God.

> *And dust returns to the ground it came from, and the spirit returns to God who gave it....* (Ecclesiastes 12:7)

It is the body that sleeps, awaiting the resurrection.

> *Listen, I tell you a great mystery: we will not all sleep, but we will all be changed—in a flash, in the twinkling of an eye, at the last trumpet. For the trumpet will sound, the dead will be raised imperishable, and we will be changed.* (1 Corinthians 15:51-52)

There Will Be a Heavenly Reunion

The hardest thing about death is separation from our loved ones, but Jesus said that all men will be reunited—some in heaven and others in hell (see Luke 13:29, 16:22-23, 27-28).

There Will Be an Eternal Blessing

God will give us new, glorified bodies:

> *But our citizenship is in heaven. And we eagerly await a Saviour from there, the Lord Jesus Christ, who, by the power that enables him to bring everything under his control, will transform our lowly bodies so that they will be like his glorious body.* (Philippians 3:20-21)

The Bible says that the body we place in the cemetery is like a seed awaiting the harvest (1 Corinthians 15:35-38, 42-44). Of course, the body turns to dust and becomes a part of nature. Nowhere in the Bible are we taught that God raises again every particle of the believer's body. The Bible teaches that the resurrected body has identity with the body that was buried, just as the seeds that come from one seed that was planted and died in the ground have identity and continuity with that seed.

Yes, it is painful to be separated from our loved ones. But let's remember that, for the believer in Jesus, death is only a temporary separation. Look at this conversation between Martha and Jesus in John 11:23-27.

Jesus said to her, *"Your brother will rise again."* Martha answered, *"I know he will rise again in the resurrection at the last day."* Jesus said to her, *"I am the resurrection and the life. He who believes in me will live, even though he dies; and whoever lives and believes in me will never die. Do you believe this?"* "Yes, Lord," she told him, *"I believe that you are the Christ, the Son of God, who has come into the world."*

Do you believer this, dear reader, or do you have some doubts? Jesus said, *"He who believes in me will live!"*

Our Soul Is Immortal
Reading: Philippians 1

In July 2000, my family had four funerals in about two weeks. Although the pain of separation was there, our hearts rejoiced and God's peace filled our hearts because we knew that each one went to a better place to meet their Creator and Lord whom they loved.

Believers in Jesus are not exempt from pain and sorrow. They can and do feel sadness and shed tears when a loved one dies. Even Jesus cried when one of His best friends died, as we read in John 11:32-36. But believers are not to grieve as the unbelievers of the world do! Why not? Because at death, the spirit of the believing Christian immediately enters the presence of the Lord!

Physical death is passing from life on earth with Christ to life in heaven with Him. Death does not interrupt the continuity of one's relationship with God—it only enriches it. The Apostle Paul said:

> *To be with Christ is far better.* (Philippians 1:23)

and...

> *We are confident, I say, and would prefer to be away from the body and at home with the Lord.* (2 Corinthians 5:8)

Yes, we all must go through the valley of the shadow of death. "Go through"... but not stay there! Our bodies are mortal, but Jesus said:

> *"I tell you the truth, if a man keeps my word, he will never see death."* (John 8:51)

The Bible makes it very clear that death is not the end. Our soul is immortal—it never dies. God created man from the dust of the ground... but that was not enough. God had to give him life so,

> *He breathed into his nostrils the breath of life, and man became a living being.* (Genesis 2:7)

The breath of God made us living beings with a soul that never dies.

> *And the dust returns to the ground it came from, and the spirit returns to God who gives it.* (Ecclesiastes 12:7)

Because Jesus conquered death, our last enemy, the Christian believer can confront death both realistically and with victory. Though death is inevitable and often unexpected, it should never completely catch us off guard. Death should never be the "great unknown" that produces fear and terror. Rather, it should be the moment when we no longer see *"through a glass, darkly"* but *"face to face"* (1 Corinthians 13:12).

Jesus said:

> *"I am the resurrection and life. He who believes in me will live, even though he dies."* (John 11:25)

And then Jesus asked Martha: *"Do you believe this?"*

Dear reader, Jesus is asking you the same question: "Do you believe that, even though you die, you will live through Jesus Christ the Saviour?" Have you invited Jesus Christ to be your Lord and Saviour? I hope you have, for only He can give you eternal life.

Eternity

Reading: John 14

The concept of eternity is one that has often made my mind race and made me feel anxious. It has caused me to cry out to God to help me deal with the idea of endless existence. When I was a young boy, thoughts of eternity and infinity would rob me of sleep, making my heart beat fast and my palms get wet.

Although the Lord helped me deal with this later on, I still think about eternity and infinity sometimes. However, now I thank God for who He is, for what He has done and is doing in my life and for how much He cares for each human being that He created. And, yes, I still think that eternity and infinity are awesome concepts.

When the Bible speaks of eternal life, it refers to our relationship with God, not just the passing of time. Jesus said:

> *"Now this is eternal life: that they may know the only true God, and Jesus Christ, whom you have sent."* (John 17:3)

Yet eternity refers to an existence that will never end. The question is where we will spend that existence. In God's presence... or with those who have rejected Christ and with the angels of darkness?

Every moment, every heartbeat brings us closer to the inevitable. We are all moving through time toward eternity. Does that fill us with joyful expectancy or with the sense of fear and anxiety?

That all depends on our relationship to Jesus Christ. Jesus has provided the only way to God. He told His disciples:

> *"I am the way and the truth and the life. No one comes to the Father except through me."* (John 14:6)

What about you? Do you know where you will spend eternity? If you don't know, or if you are not sure, please invite Jesus into your life. He is the only way to eternal life.

Shaped by the Master's Hand

"He who began a good work in you will carry it to completion...."

(Philippians 1:6)

A Strange Marriage

Reading: Romans 12

The wedding was great. People were very kind and gracious with their congratulations and greetings. The huge cake was just enough for everyone. The beautiful and generous gifts had all been opened and taken home already. Soon the limousine with the bride and groom was heading toward the airport so the newly married couple could go on their honeymoon.

Suddenly the bride turned to her new husband and said, "Chris, I want you to take me home!"

He was very surprised but managed to calmly respond: "Our house will only be ready in three weeks, when we will have returned from our honeymoon."

"No," she said, "I don't mean the house you are building for me. I mean my house. I want to return to my old home." Chris was shocked. She was serious!

His bride continued, "Chris, I am glad that I married you. We now belong to each other and, whenever I want, I can use your name as my name. But I want to go back to my old house. Now that we are married, I will be seeing you from time to time, but to stay with you continually? Forget it. I want to go back home, to my friends, my activities, my life. Of course, I love you. I took you as my husband, didn't I? I will belong to you forever, but I don't want you to interfere with my life. I will live as I please. When I am sick or have problems, I will naturally call you to come and help. You are my husband, no matter what. Thank you for loving me and for asking me to be your bride… but this is my life and I will do whatever I want."

This would not be a marriage, would it? It would be a mockery of the vows that were made... a terrible joke!

Just as marriage is an act of total commitment, so is becoming a born-again Christian. There are many who call themselves Christians but whose actions and attitudes do not differ from the attitude of this bride.

They say with their lives: "Lord, I received You as my own Saviour. Thank You for saving me. But, now, please leave me alone. I will go back to my friends, and I will live as I was living before. If I need Your help, I will ask You for it. After all, You are my Saviour, right? But don't ask me to live just as You want me to... that is going a little too far! Of course, when I die I want to come to the house that You are preparing for me, but until then, let me live the way I want to."

If this is my attitude, am I a Christian? Have I given my heart completely to Christ?

In Romans 7, we see what happens when we become born-again Christians. In fact, Paul uses the analogy of marriage to describe our union with Christ.

Are you His and is He yours?

> *Therefore, I urge you brothers, in view of God's mercy, to offer your bodies as living sacrifices, holy and pleasing to God—which is your spiritual worship.* (Romans 12:1)

Committed or Gone Fishing?

Reading: John 21:1-19

For a human relationship to be successful, effective and lasting, you need unconditional love and commitment.

Today, more than ever before, most relationships are temporary, unpredictable and unreliable. Commitments are conditional and usually depend on circumstances and feelings. As the mood changes, so does the commitment. Short-lived relationships have become a way of life. This goes for relationships between husband and wife, between family members, between friends and even between man and God.

The truth is, we do not naturally possess, nor are we capable of producing, the kind of pure, unselfish and unconditional love that is necessary in relationships. Only God can give us that kind of love... because God IS love.

> *And so we know and rely on the love God has for us. God is love. Whoever lives in love lives in God, and God in him.* (1 John 4:16)

> *"For God so loved the world that He gave His one and only Son, that whoever believes in Him shall not perish but have eternal life."* (John 3:16)

The world cannot understand this kind of love and the conversation between Jesus and Peter in John 21:15-19 would have been terribly misunderstood today. Jesus asks, *"Simon, do you love me more than these?"* Peter responds, *"Yes, Lord, you know that I love you."*

To really understand Jesus' question, we must put it in its right context. Jesus had spent three years with His disciples. He, like a good shepherd, had given them everything they needed... including His own life. He had made a commitment and honoured it—but they had all broken their promises to Him.

They had promised to follow Him to the end. Peter had proudly said, "Even if all fall away... I never will. Even if I have to die with You, I will never disown You." A few hours later, one disciple betrayed Jesus, the others ran for their lives and Peter denied Him three times.

But Jesus did not stop loving them. He kept His promise and He went to meet them. He even prepared breakfast for them (John 21:12). Jesus had given them instructions to wait for Him and continue in their ministry, but they decided to go fishing instead. When He came to them, they didn't even notice Him.

Is it any wonder, then, that Jesus asked Peter the same question three times? *"Simon, do you love me more than these?"* Each time that Peter said, *"I love you, Lord,"* Jesus reminded Peter that he should put his love into action.

Jesus is asking us, He is asking you, the same question today: *"Do you love me more than these?"* Do you love God and His Son who died for you more than the other things in your life? If so, His last command to Peter is the same for you: *"Follow me."*

Wanted: Full-time, Permanent Christians

Reading: Joshua 24:14-27

Anyone in the work force will recognize the terms "full time", "part time", "temporary" and "permanent". They refer to how often and for how long one is expected to work at their job.

Jesus could have used these same terms to describe His followers. His disciples and a group of women were full-time followers (Luke 9:1). He also appointed seventy-two part-time workers (Luke 10:1). You could even say that Jesus had occasional followers: the crowds of people who wanted to hear Him speak (Luke 9:11). After the Pentecost, the Church grew rapidly and, although some people could have been labelled part-time or occasional workers, most were full-time followers of Christ and their numbers were growing daily (Acts 2:41).

Today's Christians can be categorized in the same manner.

FULL-TIME, PERMANENT CHRISTIANS

> *Therefore, my dear brothers, stand firm. Let nothing move you. Always give yourselves fully to the work of the Lord, because you know that your labor in the Lord is not in vain.* (1 Corinthians 15:58)

PART-TIME CHRISTIANS

> *You cannot drink the cup of the Lord and the cup of demons, too; you cannot have a part in both the Lord's table and the table of demons.* (1 Corinthians 10:21)

OCCASIONAL CHRISTIANS

> *For he had healed many, so that those with diseases were pushed forward to touch Him.* (Mark 3:10)

TEMPORARY CHRISTIANS

> *From this time many of his disciples turned back and no longer followed him....* (John 6:66)

What kind of believers does God want? Do we have our choice of category?

> *And now what does the Lord your God ask of you but to fear the Lord your God, to walk in all his ways, to love him, to serve the Lord your God with all your heart and with all your soul, and to observe the Lord's commands and decrees that I am giving you today for your own good?* (Deuteronomy 10:12-13)

Sounds like God wants the full-time, permanent types. The only categories we can choose from are God and evil (Joshua 24:14-15). There really can be no part-time, occasional or temporary Christians. Such people only deceive themselves. To those who put their work and play first, Christ says,

> *"No one who puts his hand to the plough and looks back is fit for service in the kingdom of God."* (Luke 9:62)

Before pointing out a "part-time Christian" that you know, check what category you fit in yourself. Can you honestly call yourself a full-time and permanent Christian?

> *"If anyone would come after me, he must deny himself and take up his cross daily and follow me. For whoever wants to save his life will lose it, but whoever loses his life for me will save it."* (Luke 9:23-24)

God wants full-time workers!

Keep the Words

Reading: Revelation 22:7-21

In the past few years I have been buying many books on health and healthy eating. I have read most of them and have found them to be helpful. Most of them make a lot of sense. However, although I like the books and the detailed instructions in them, I have to admit that I have not always put into practice the advice given in these guides. I am not "keeping the words" of the books I read.

Many people read books, enjoy them, recommend them to others and even defend them… but they themselves don't adhere to what the books say. This is the same for many who read the Bible but don't "keep the words" in it. Of course, to be able to do the things we read we must first understand them.

Revelation 22:7 begins with the word "behold". This is an order to look, to pay attention. Then Jesus says, *"I am coming soon!"* and He repeats that in verses 12 and 20: *"Yes, I am coming soon."* It may be sooner than we think. It may be today or tomorrow or a few years from now. In any case, each one of us will see Him, either when He returns or when we are called home.

Jesus makes another thing very clear: that only those who keep His words will be blessed. In other words, only those who read the Bible and obey it will be blessed. God has said many things in the Bible, but we will focus on Jesus' words in Revelation 22:7-21.

First, though, let's take a look at John's report of what the angel said on behalf of God.

> *I, John, am the one who heard and saw these things. And when I had heard and seen them, I fell down to worship at the feet of the angel who had been showing them to me. But he said to me, "Do not do it! I am a fellow servant with you and with your brothers the prophets and of all who keep the words of this book. Worship God!"* (Revelation 22:8-9)

"Worship God." This order goes all the way back to the Ten Commandments. We are not to worship angels. We are not to worship saints, teachings or doctrines. Anything we put before Jesus Christ is an idol. We cannot even make anything else equal with God.

That's what is so subtle about those who put so many other things with or ahead of God. They talk and preach about the Church, the saints, Mary, and Christ's teachings... but you can't find Jesus Christ in their lives even if you search with a flashlight.

You would have to get past the men, women, angels, religion, customs and doctrines before you found Christ.

> *"Behold, I am coming soon! My reward is with me, and I will give to everyone according to what he has done."* (Revelation 22:12)

This is not teaching salvation by works, but rather works as the fruit and proof of salvation. Jesus is reminding His followers to not practise sin. He wants us to keep our robes, which He washed with His blood, clean. Jesus is telling us to "keep the words of this book." Don't just read them. Live them.

Grow in Grace

Reading: 2 Peter 3

The Christian life, like the physical life, begins with a birth. When we accept Christ as our Saviour, we are "born-again".

> *Yet to all who received him, to those who believed in his name, he gave the right to become children of God—children born not of natural descent, nor of human decision or a husband's will, but born of God.* (John 1:12-13)

Once the new birth takes place, one must grow in grace. What does this mean? It is not becoming "more saved" than at the moment of conversion. It is not becoming more pardoned, more justified. Growing in grace means there is an increase in the degree, size, strength, vigour and power of the grace that the Holy Spirit brings into a believer's heart. But what is the evidence of growth?

An Increase of Love Toward Others

> *May the Lord make your love increase and overflow for each other and for everyone else, just as ours does for you.* (1 Thessalonians 3:12)

> *"By this all men will know that you are my disciples, if you love one another."* (John 13:35)

An Increase of Faith

> *We ought always to thank God for you, brothers, and rightly so, because your faith is growing more and more, and the love every one of you has for each other is increasing.* (2 Thessalonians 1:3)

An Increase of Knowledge of God

> *And we pray this in order that you may live a life worthy of the Lord and may please him in every way: bearing fruit in every good work, growing in the knowledge of God.* (Colossians 1:10)

A Greater Desire for Holiness

> *Brothers, I do not consider myself yet to have taken hold of it. But one thing I do: Forgetting what is behind and straining toward what is ahead.* (Philippians 3:13)

What are some things through which God helps us grow in grace? He uses His Word (1 Peter 2:2), our troubles (Romans 5), our quiet time with Him, worship services, fellowship with other believers, etc.

Just as we expect a baby to grow up and mature, a tree to grow and be fruitful, an investment to mature and bring profit... so must we as Christians grow, mature and be fruitful! Are you growing in grace?

Are You Growing?

Reading: Hebrews 5:11-6:3

Melissa's mother was very happy. Her daughter was growing up so fast and could now walk, eat and dress all by herself. One day, Melissa's mother decided, "I will take Melissa to daycare so she can learn to speak better and be prepared to start school."

A few months later, Melissa was able to communicate well with the toddlers at the daycare and she seemed to be very happy. However, her mother noticed that, instead of speaking better and learning more words, her child was forgetting the words she already knew and was using "baby talk" again!

Why? What was happening? Well, it was simply this: Melissa was surrounded with younger children and babies and was picking up their baby talk and expressions. The situation was not too difficult to correct. Melissa would be moved to a school where she would learn from knowledgeable teachers rather than mimic babies.

Apostle Paul, writing to Jewish believers, said:

> *Even though by this time you ought to be teachers, you need someone to teach you the elementary truths of God's word all over again. You need milk, not solid food.* (Hebrews 5:12)

Paul was telling them that they should have been mature enough to teach others, but they were still babes in Christ. They were like nursing infants, lacking spiritual fruit and in danger of severe discipline from the Lord. He warned them to put away childish things and to grow up.

Later, in Hebrews 6:1, he told them *"to leave the elementary teachings about Christ and go on to maturity, and perfection."* He told them to leave the milk stage and grow up to full age by feeding on the solid food of the Word.

So many churches today have the same problem. Instead of being equipping centres, helping new believers grow spiritually, they are just nurseries for spiritual babes and toddlers who enjoy remaining immature, and thus neglect the rest of the family of God.

Obviously, a growing church needs to feed and nurture new believers with the Word of God, but it must be with the goal of yielding mature Christians. And these new Christians who have matured and been equipped will teach other new believers who come in.

What about you? Have you grown since you became a follower of Christ? Are you eating solid spiritual food or are you still drinking milk? Are you sure you are growing spiritually?

Apostle Peter ended his letter to the believers this way:

> *But grow in the grace and knowledge of our Lord and Saviour Jesus Christ.* (2 Peter 3:18)

Is it time for you to graduate from spiritual daycare?

Growth Is a Must
Reading: 1 Peter 2:1-12

Those of us who have children in our families or who work with children must be concerned at one time or another about a child's physical or mental growth. We may wonder why a child is not growing fast enough or why he or she is not walking or talking yet. I have done that with our children and do it with our grandchildren even though my wife reassures me that they are doing fine. It seems I am too anxious to see them grow and do well.

The normal, healthy growth of children is the desire of every parent and of society in general. The tragedy of children not growing is a great concern to doctors and parents alike.

Birth… growth… maturity. These are goals in our physical life. What about in our spiritual, Christian life? There, too, we should see birth, growth and maturity.

Just as a healthy newborn baby hungers for food, so should the Christian believer eagerly desire spiritual food and growth. The word "therefore" in 1 Peter 2:1 connects with verse 23 of the previous verse:

> *For you have been born again, not of perishable seed, but of imperishable, through the living and enduring word of God: Therefore…. Like newborn babies, crave pure spiritual milk, so that you may grow up in your salvation.*

Many children want to hold on to the things they cherish but it is natural for these to be put away with maturity. Apostle Paul said:

> *When I was a child, I talked like a child, I thought like a child, I reasoned like a child. When I became a man, I put childish ways behind me.* (1 Corinthians 13:11)

Apostle Peter lists some of the things that we should put away:

> *Therefore, rid yourselves of all malice and all deceit, hypocrisy, envy and slander of every kind.* (1 Peter 2:1)

We should put away these things and feed on the things that will help us mature spiritually. We need proper food for proper growth and are effected by what we take in. What are you feeding your mind? Your heart? Your soul?

Some things are bad for or useless to our spiritual growth. Much of today's reading material and television is full of profanity, violence, greed, unnatural ways of life, and meaningless things that leave the human heart empty and hungry. They stunt growth and destroy the human spirit. Even religion cannot satisfy the heart... only God can. God's Word brings spiritual growth and fills the heart.

Many Christians are atrophic, wasting away, starving to spiritual death... and they either don't know it or they don't care. Eventually, they will develop spiritual anorexia, completely losing their appetite and risking death if not treated.

Unless a baby is fed and nourished, no matter how warm, safe and secure he is kept, he will not grow and will eventually die. The same applies to adults: no matter how clean you keep yourself and exercise, you will eventually become weak and be in danger of dying unless you eat and nourish your body.

In the same way, no matter how "clean" you are doctrinally and how busy you are with religious activities, unless you are fed spiritually with the Word of God, you will not grow and mature.

How is your spiritual appetite? Is it your desire to grow spiritually and become a mature and happy believer?

Marks of Maturity

Reading: Ephesians 4:7-16

The word "maturity" usually describes ripeness, being full grown or developed, or being due. We refer to fruit and crops as being mature when they are ready to be eaten or harvested. We call people mature when they reach a certain age or level of physical and mental development. Maturity also describes the condition of being completed or ready.

What is Christian maturity? God's general plan for us is birth, growth and maturity. This principle also applies to our spiritual lives.

Some of the characteristics of spiritual infancy are: being more concerned with self than with service and godliness, being more concerned with arguments than with actions, and being more interested in people than in God. But how do we recognize Christian maturity?

In Ephesians 4:11, "to prepare" means to mature. The King James Version uses the word "perfecting". God has given gifts to the Church to help us mature. Prophets and apostles, with their writings, have established and helped the Church to grow and mature. Pastors and teachers have the primary responsibility of bringing about spiritual growth.

Sadly, many misunderstand the role of the pastor. Many pastors have become the ones who do the work of the ministry instead of maturing and equipping others to do it. And most Christians, instead of being participants, have become spectators, enjoying the ride. However, mature believers see their mission in life as doing the work of the ministry: reaching out to others with the love and gospel of their Lord.

Christ is the head of the Church and every believer is a member of the Body of Christ. What can you do to build up the Body?

You can care for parts of the Body that are afflicted. You can pray for the sick and help them. You can visit the fatherless, motherless and widowed.

> *Religion that God our Father accepts as pure and faultless is this: to look after orphans and widows in their distress and to keep oneself from being polluted by the world.* (James 1:27)

Sadly, many of these responsibilities have been shifted to social services.

Consider whether others have become stronger because of you. Is the Body more unified because of you? Ephesians 4:14 tells us that we are, or should be, solid in doctrine. Do you know why you believe what you believe? Maturity in the Word of God brings maturity in life.

We must examine ourselves for the marks of maturity! In what areas are your greatest needs for growth?

With Wings as Eagles
Reading: Isaiah 40:28-31

The Bible is full of metaphors that are used to help people understand a message and to understand themselves. Some of these are, for example, sheep (John 10:1-5), salt (Matthew 5:13), light (Matthew 5:14), branches (John 15:5), vapour (James 4:14) and soldiers (Ephesians 6:11).

In Isaiah 40, the true believer in God is also compared to the greatest of birds: the eagle. There are at least three applications we can find in this analogy:

THE EAGLE IS KNOWN FOR ITS STRENGTH

A true Christian should be strong in the Lord.

> *Therefore my brothers, stand firm. Let nothing move you.* (1 Corinthians 15:58)

A true Christian should also never be "weary in doing good" (Galatians 6:9). Being physically tired is natural, but we must never give up on doing good to others.

A true believer is not a "wimp" or weak person. On the contrary, we have all the spiritual strength we need in the Lord.

The Eagle Rises Above the World

… which is trapped by gases, smoke, dust and all kinds of other pollutants. The Christian rises above the filthy things of the world.

> *Set your minds on things above, not on earthly things.*
> (Colossians 3:2)

The true Christian may walk on the earth, but his or her mind should be far above the clouds.

> *After that, we who are still alive and are left will be caught up together with them in the clouds to meet the Lord in the air. And so we will be with the Lord forever.*
> (1 Thessalonians 4:17)

The Eagle Is Known for Its Longevity

The Christian whose name is written in the Book of Life will live forever. King David wrote,

> *Surely goodness and love will follow me all the days of my life, and I will dwell in the house of the Lord forever.*
> (Psalm 23:6)

How strong are you, dear Christian believer? How far-sighted are you? How high have you risen above the world and its corrupt system?

Your answers to these questions determine the kind of Christian you are. Are you like an eagle? If your answer is, "I would like to be, but I am not strong enough," please listen to what Isaiah said:

He gives strength to the weary and increases the power of the weak. Even youths grow tired and weary, and young men stumble and fall; but those who hope in the Lord will renew their strength. They will soar on wings like eagles; they will run and not grow weary, they will walk and not be faint. (Isaiah 40:29-31)

Power, Love and Discipline
Reading: 2 Timothy 1

There is a misconception in the world that believing in God, Jesus, heaven and hell, and life after death and following Christ's teachings faithfully is a sign of weakness and the result of being timid, fearful, insecure, unhappy and not very intelligent or, as many would say, "wimpy".

Little does the world know that it is completely the opposite. The born-again believer no longer relies only on his own strength and abilities but, being connected to the source of all power, wisdom and love, enjoys the supernatural pleasures and gifts that come from God through His Holy Spirit.

For God did not give us a spirit of timidity, but a spirit of power, of love and of self-discipline. So do not be ashamed to testify about our Lord. (2 Timothy 1:7-8)

Here Apostle Paul is talking about the Holy Spirit, who indwells the true believer. The Holy Spirit does not generate fear in us, but rather he brings power, love and discipline. Every believer needs all three.

God gives us, through the Holy Spirit, a spirit of *power*. Unlimited strength is at our disposal. Apostle Paul is writing this letter to Timothy while he is in prison and is about to be martyred. Now, does Paul sound like a timid man? Not at all! When a religious leader sitting safely in his ivory tower sends a letter or writes a book telling people not to worry or be afraid because they will be protected by the Spirit... that is theory.

But when someone who is in prison and about to unjustly die writes that... that is power, that is a real manifestation of power, that is experiencing the power of the Holy Spirit... not just talking about it. Through the enabling of the Holy Spirit, the believer can serve and live without fear, persevere patiently, suffer triumphantly and even die with dignity.

God has also given us a spirit of *love*. It is our love for God that drives out all fear and makes us willing to give ourselves to Christ, whatever the cost may be.

> *The fruit of the Spirit is love....* (Galatians 5:22)

Our love for Christ, for the Word of God, for other believers and for the unbelievers comes from the Holy Spirit.

> *God has poured out his love into our hearts by the Holy Spirit, whom he has given us.* (Romans 5:5)

In fact, it is our love for our fellow man that makes us willing to endure all kinds of persecutions and abuses and to repay them with kindness. If you are filled with the Spirit of God, then you know what I am talking about.

The Holy Spirit also gives us *discipline* and self-control. We must use discretion and not act rashly or foolishly. No matter what the circumstances, we should act carefully and "keep our cool". This kind of discipline does not come easily or naturally. Our nature says, "Act quickly!" and our responses are usually based on our emotions rather than on logic or love.

Our best example of someone demonstrating all three characteristics—power, love and discipline—is, of course, Jesus

Christ. But many others have followed in His footsteps. The question is, "Are we as the Church and as individuals walking in His footsteps? Are you experiencing the Holy Spirit's power, love and discipline in you?"

If yes, praise the Lord. If you're not sure or don't know how to receive this power, remember Jesus' words:

> *You will receive power when the Holy Spirit comes on you.* (Acts 1:8)

And we receive the Holy Spirit only by being born-again, through the new birth.

The Journey of Life
Reading: 1 John 1:5-6:11

Life is a journey. It starts at birth and ends at death. Some go through it unwillingly, others are dragged or pushed and still others refuse to go on and abruptly terminate their journey. Then there are those who, regardless of the difficulties they face, make that journey to the end—and not only do they enjoy the journey themselves, but they help others enjoy it, too!

You and I are on a journey. We can take this walk alone or be in the company of others. The question is, what kind of company? Life, for many, is like a walk down a dark alley in the company of unhappy people who do not know where they are going. For others, life is like walking down a well-lit street in the company of friends and with the continuous help of a guide who knows the way to the end.

Life, at best, is a rough road. Life without God is a rough, dark and dangerous road to travel on. In the presence of God, who *"is the Light*" (1 John 1:5), and the help of the Holy Spirit who is our Guide, our journey of life becomes a wonderful experience.

King David proclaimed:

> *The Lord is my light and my salvation—whom shall I fear?* (Psalm 27:1)

and later:

> *Your word is a lamp to my feet and a light for my path.* (Psalm 119:105)

No wonder the path of the believer becomes wonderful when God is present! In other words, God is light, safety and life. Satan is darkness, insecurity and death.

> *The god of this age has blinded the minds of unbelievers, so that they cannot see the light of the gospel of the Glory of Christ, who is the image of God.* (2 Corinthians 4:4)

Now, those who obey God walk in the light, but those who disobey God walk in darkness! In the presence of God, there is no darkness. However, in 1 John 1:5-10 and 2:1-6, John points out that it is possible for people to say that they are in the light and yet live in darkness. Let's look at the four lies in these passages:

LYING ABOUT OUR NATURE—saying that we have no sin (1 John 1:8).

LYING ABOUT OUR DEEDS—saying that we do not sin and, therefore, confession is not needed (1 John 1:9).

LYING ABOUT OUR COMMITMENT TO GOD—saying that we know God and keep His commandments when we do not.

> *The man who says, "I know him," but does not do what he commands is a liar, and the truth is not in him.*

Whoever claims to live in him must walk as Jesus did. 1 John 2:4,6)

Lying about Our Fellowship with God and with Others.

God has promised to fellowship with all those who call on Him in truth (Psalm 145:18). Fellowship with one another is not an option—even Jesus needed it. The early believers recognized their need for fellowship (Acts 2:46-47).

It is sad to see many professing Christians talk about spiritual things but not walk in the Spirit and Light.

Walk in the Light

Reading: Ephesians 5:1-21

The Apostle Paul, in writing to the believers in Ephesus, reminded them what they were before they believed in Jesus:

For you were once darkness, but now you are light in the Lord. (Ephesians 5:8)

He did not say they were *in* darkness. He said they *were* darkness.

What is darkness? It is the lack of light. It doesn't take anything to have darkness, but it takes energy to have light. You may have the best lighting system at home, but unless it is connected to an electrical power source, you will have darkness.

We were darkness at one time because we were not connected, plugged into the power source. Jesus said:

> "I am the light of the world. Whoever follows me will never walk in darkness, but will have the light of the life." (John 8:12)

The result of being plugged in or connected to the source of light is being light. If you are a true believer and a follower of Jesus, then you are connected to the source of absolute power and you are LIGHT!

We are either light or darkness. We can't be both—it is impossible. The light cannot compromise with the darkness; it can only expose it.

> *This is the message we have heard from him and declare to you: God is light; in Him there is no darkness at all. If we claim to have fellowship with Him yet walk in the darkness, we lie and do not live by the truth. But if we walk in the light, as He is in the light, we have fellowship with one another, and the blood of Jesus, His Son, purifies us from all sin.* (1 John 1:5-7)

Don't Look Back!

Reading: Luke 9:57-62

In writing this, I had to ask myself some questions and then try to find the answers. This was not an easy process because there are times and circumstances that make it necessary to look back. For example, while backing up your vehicle, when trying to remember something from the past, when taking stock of your inventory in business to know how much merchandise to reorder, etc.—these are times you have to look back. The truth is, though, that you cannot go very far if you are always looking backward instead of forward while walking, running or driving.

> *"No one who puts his hand to the plough and looks back is fit for service in the kingdom of God."* (Luke 9:62)

Looking back hinders progress; it may depress you and it may bring defeat. There are five things we must not look back at:

SINS THAT HAVE BEEN FORGIVEN

1 John 1:7-9 gives us the guarantee of forgiveness for our sins. God really does put our sins away (see also Psalm 103:3, 12). It may be that you believe this to be true for others but not for yourself. But you must believe and accept that God has forgiven and put away all your sins, even your most serious ones.

DEFEATS THAT GET YOU DOWN

Everyone has been defeated at some time in his or her past. Only those who never attempt anything are free from failure. But God lifts up those who fall (Psalm 27:23-24).

A PAST THAT SEEMS BETTER THAN IT REALLY WAS

> *Do not say, "Why were the old days better than these?" For it is not wise to ask such questions.* (Ecclesiastes 7:10)

But the Israelites did just that. They looked back toward Egypt and complained (Numbers 11:17,20). The present never seems to be as good as the past. The truth is, however, that a great future beats a great past every time.

OLD CONFLICTS THAT MAKE YOU BITTER

Every time we relive old conflicts, the hurt returns. Even those forgiven and resolved conflicts can become dangerous again if we keep going over them. We must forget the past and get on with living and growing (1 Peter 2:1-2).

OLD VICTORIES THAT MAKE YOU THINK YOU'VE GOT IT MADE

I have heard people say things like, "Oh, I served the Lord with all my heart… once. I was a soul winner… once. I was close to Christ… once." But what about today? Hebrews 12:2 tells us to fix our eyes on Jesus! Look to the fields and start caring for others… and you will forget the past as you serve others.

Friends, let's look ahead. The best is yet to come!

Three Kinds of People

Reading: 1 Corinthians 2:14-3:4

There are all kinds of sermons. Some are directed to unbelievers and the aim is to convert the lost. Others are directed to believers with the goal of feeding or correcting them. Well, this message is for you… no matter what kind of person you think you are.

There are three kinds of people. You may agree or disagree, but every one of us fits into one of these three descriptions:

THE NATURAL PERSON (1 Corinthians 2:14)

Apostle Paul wanted to reach the "natural man" and his message was *"Jesus Christ and Him crucified."* But who is the natural man?

The natural man is the person who has not received the gift of God—salvation through Jesus Christ. It is the person who has not been born-again. The natural person cannot understand spiritual things; they are foolishness to him. The Bible is a dark book to the natural person, his destiny is distraction and his need is salvation.

All people are naturally lost (Romans 3:23), but all people can be saved (John 6:37; Romans 10:13)!

THE SPIRITUAL PERSON (1 Corinthians 2:15)

The spiritual person was once a natural person but, through faith in Jesus Christ, he or she was transformed and is now a new person. Once doomed, this person is now saved; once lost, now found; once bound for hell, now bound for heaven.

The spiritual person learns from the Holy Spirit and is able to discern and understand spiritual things. The spiritual person sees God at work in the world and in his or her own life. This person is often not understood by others, but Jesus predicted that in John 15:18-20. The spiritual person has the mind of Christ.

THE CARNAL PERSON (1 Corinthians 3:1)

The carnal person is a baby in Christ. Whereas the natural person lives for the moment and the spiritual person lays up treasures in heaven, the carnal person looks both ways. The carnal person knows what is right but doesn't do it. He knows the world is lost but sticks to it as if his life depended upon it. He is like Lot who wasted his time by lingering in Sodom.

The carnal person, who resembles the detestably "lukewarm" church in Laodicea (Revelation 3:15-16), needs a full commitment to Christ.

Which kind of person are *you*? Remember that Christ will meet you where you are and make you the spiritual person you ought to be... but it's your move now.

> *Everyone who calls on the name of the Lord will be saved.* (Romans 10:13)

The Believer's Life
Reading: 1 Peter 1:3-25

Being a member of a Christian church or claiming to be a Christian does not make someone a Christian. A true Christian is a person who not only claims to be a follower of Christ, but one who also *lives* Christ in his or her earthly life.

The kind of life a true believer lives is what separates him or her in this hostile world. The true believer's life has or must have three distinctions.

A Life of Hope (1 Peter 1:3-12)

This world offers no lasting hope. As sinners, we had no hope beyond the grave. We were under the sentence of death, hopelessly lost. But Jesus Christ, in His great mercy, paid the penalty of our sins.

> *Remember that at that time you were separate from Christ… without hope and without God in the world. But now in Christ Jesus you who once were far away have been brought near through the blood of Christ.* (Ephesians 2:12-13)

The believer has a living hope because he has a living Saviour. It is not only a living hope, but also a lasting hope. When we are born-again, we have the sure hope of an inheritance in heaven that can never perish, spoil or fade.

A Life of Holiness (1 Peter 1:13-21)

The blessed hope should make us live holy lives.

> *Everyone who has this hope in him purifies himself, just as he is pure.* (1 John 3:3)

In 1 Peter 1:16, "holy" does not mean sinless perfection—a condition that is impossible in this life. 1 John 1:8-10 explains that "holy" means set apart, separated for God. Our lives as believers should emulate the holy character of God. We must be holy in all we do and say! We must make a clean break with the corrupt world system from which Christ died to deliver us.

We are in the world but not of the world. This does not mean that we must isolate ourselves from sinners; rather, we must bring the Good News to them. Yet, in our dealings and relationships with them, we must never share in or condone their sins. We must show by our lives that we are children of God.

The moment we become like the world, our testimony is weakened. Why would unbelievers want to become Christians if they cannot see a difference, a change for the better in our lives?

Being holy does not imply passive inactivity, and it does not come easy or naturally. You have to fight for it.

> *Therefore, prepare your minds for action....* (1 Peter 1:13)

Living a holy life is not optional—it is a command! The great need today is for Christians to live separated, holy, dedicated lives for the glory of God. Many Christians are so worldly that their testimony (if they have one) is meaningless. If a testimony of salvation is not backed up by a corresponding life, it does more harm than good.

A Life of Harmony (1 Peter 1:22-25)

Salvation gives us a living hope, a desire for a holy life and a wonderful fellowship with the people of God. The Apostle Peter once again reminds us that, because we are born-again into the family of God through Christ, we must love as He loved us all.

One of the things this new birth brings into our lives is love! Loving is not optional either. It is part of the Christian life and character. True, unselfish Christian love brings harmony to the Church and to the believers themselves.

King David wrote,

> *How good and pleasant it is when brothers live together in unity.* (Psalm 133:1)

The Bible says that the outward evidence our salvation is the love we have toward each other. Not "friendship" love, not "I like you" love, not even "I am in love with you" love—these kinds of love are found and practised in the world, too. Pure, unselfish Christian love does not come naturally. It is not part of our human nature. This love is a special kind of love that comes, or must come, with the new birth.

> *Now that you have purified yourselves by obeying the truth so that you have sincere love for your brothers, love one another deeply, from the heart. For you have been born again, not of perishable seed, but of imperishable, through the living and enduring word of God.* (1 Peter 1:22-23)

People around us will know we are true followers of Christ by our love, not by our words alone.

> *"A new command I give you: Love one another. As I have loved you, so you must love one another. By this all men will know that you are my disciples if you love one another."* (John 13:34-35)

The Christian life is a life of hope, holiness and harmony. Only one, or even two of three, will not do.

Hindrances to Faith

Reading: Galatians 1:1-9; 5:16-26

I believe that finding God and trusting in Jesus is easier than deciphering and understanding religious legalism and practices. Jesus had a simple message for His followers—a message of love and hope from God to the human race. Those who trusted Jesus and accepted this Good News were transformed and received eternal life and God's blessings. As human nature goes, however, people started adding to this simple message to make it more impressive and complicated, thus obscuring God's message which is simple enough for all to understand.

In the New Testament, we see thousands of people responding positively to the gospel and many churches being established. When the Apostle Paul wrote to the church in Galatia, he used six sad words to describe the condition of their congregation: *"You were running a good race."* These words speak of: (a) past blessings and (b) present failure. Paul obviously felt that the church was no longer running well.

The hindrances that caused the decline of the Galatian church included:

FALSE TEACHING

False teachers had come to confuse the Galatians. They didn't care about the lost—they went to those already trusting in Christ and presented a false message, *"a different gospel"* (Galatians 1:6). Those who teach a message that results in the eternal destruction of souls will be doomed and lost. As Paul did not tolerate these teachings, neither should the Church, the Body of Christ.

Fighting Christians

How strange! These people wanted to be under the law, yet the very opposite was happening. They were backbiting and devouring one another (Galatians 5:15) while they knew that the law required them to love their neighbours. Believers are to show love, not hate. Love is the proof of faith in Jesus and of being His disciple (John 13:35). Strife and divisions are marks of worldliness (James 3:14-16), but peace and unity among believers is from God (James 3:17-18).

Fleshly Ambitions

The spirit and the flesh are in constant conflict. God could have removed the fleshly nature from believers at the time of their conversion, but He chose not to. Instead, He gave us His own Holy Spirit to indwell us. Things that tempt the flesh surround us, but we must not be overcome by giving in to these temptations. Rather, we must overcome them with God's help. The fruit of the Spirit should flow through us (Galatians 5:22-23). It is significant that Paul distinguishes between the *"works of the flesh"* and the *"fruit of the Spirit"*. These are as unlike as a factory and a garden.

Did you once serve Christ better than you do today? What has held you back? Throw off whatever is hindering you and let His Spirit fill your life.

Peace

Reading: Romans 5:1-11

Daily we hear about new developments, products, methods and even religions that claim to be better, faster, more reliable and more pleasurable. Nations are signing new peace treaties and new commercial agreements—almost without shame—for they know the world is becoming more and more divided and fragmented.

Tribal discords and fights are everywhere. While everyone talks about peace these days, the world is headed toward anything but peace. NATO celebrated its 50th anniversary, but war has not stopped, bombs are still falling and hundreds of thousands of refugees are fleeing their countries to find a safe place... though they are not necessarily escaping their misery.

No matter who is to blame, the fact remains that, with all the new technology and religiosity in the world, there is no peace in sight. Everyone wants to go his or her own way. Disrespect, violence and ungodliness have destroyed the family unit. Doubts and hatred have replaced love.

The Apostle Paul puts it this way: *"The way of peace they do not know"* (Romans 3:17). Why is there so little peace in the world? Why would teenagers kill each other? The Bible says that we are all born with seeds of suspicion, violence, hatred and destruction within us.

Jesus, knowing our nature, said that there are going to be wars and conflicts until the end of this age. That is, of course, until our human nature changes through the spiritual new birth. We can only experience peace when we have been forgiven by God and made things right with Him.

> *"There is no peace,"* says my God, *"for the wicked."* (Isaiah 57:21)

To those who reject God and ignore His call, the Bible says:

> *When terror comes, they will seek peace, but there will be none.* (Ezekiel 7:25)

But God sent Jesus who, through His death on the cross, made peace with God for us. He became our peace (Colossians 1:20).

There are three kinds of peace described in the Bible: peace with God, the peace of God and future peace. Peace with God can be found immediately through Jesus Christ. The peace of God enters our lives when we have made peace with Him and it sustains us through the problems and anxieties we face in life.

Finally, we will have true, lasting peace when the Prince of Peace comes… hopefully soon! When Jesus returns, those who have made Him their Lord will at last have peace. This future peace can only come to those who first make peace with God!

> *Not only is this so, but we also rejoice in God through our Lord Jesus Christ, through whom we have now received reconciliation.* (Romans 5:11)

Good Works?

Reading: James 2:14-26; Titus 3

The question about the price or method of obtaining salvation and pleasing God among those who believe in God has been a misunderstood and controversial subject. Are we saved by our good works or by God's grace?

There are those who believe and teach that man can only be saved and find peace through good works. Others believe and teach that man is saved by grace alone and that good works have nothing to do with it.

Many religious groups, both inside and outside the Christian world, misunderstand or ignore the grace of God or, as Paul puts it in 1 Peter 5:10, *"the God of all grace"*. They have adopted and proclaimed the notion that man can only be justified and saved through "good works". In other words, for a price. To me, that is just like saying to a sick man with a very bad heart to first get up and work as hard as he can for the heart transplant which he needs.

Then there are those who, realizing the error of justification by works alone, have said, correctly, that man can never be saved through his good works but by God's grace through faith.

> *For it is by grace you have been saved, through faith—and this not from yourselves, it is the gift of God. Not by works, so that no one can boast.* (Ephesians 2:8-9)

Now, where a large number of people in this second group have gone wrong (according to the Bible) is in their attitude toward good works. They say that works have *nothing* to do with salvation. They have gone to the other extreme.

I have often been asked, "What about works? Don't you think that Christians should have good works?" My answer has always been a very definite, "Yes, we should have good works!" The great emphasis of the epistle of James and Titus, chapters 2 and 3, is "good works"—but not as a means of salvation.

Because we are saved by God's mercy (Titus 3:5) and justified by His grace (Titus 3:7), we are under strict obligation to be: *"zealous of good works"* (Titus 2:14), *"an example of good works"* (Titus 2:7), *"careful to maintain good works"* (Titus 3:8,14), *"rich in good works"* (1 Timothy 6:18), *"fruitful in every good work"* (Colossians 1:10), *"prepared unto every good work"* (2 Timothy 2:21) and *"spurring one another toward good works"* (Hebrews 10:24).

Being saved by grace and then not doing good works is like the man who receives a heart transplant and then spends the rest of his life in bed doing nothing. He is as good as dead.

> *Live such good lives among the pagans that, though they accuse you of doing wrong, they may see your good deeds and glorify God on the day he visits us.* (1 Peter 2:12)

> *"In the same way, let your light shine before men, that they may see your good deeds and praise your Father in Heaven."* (Matthew 5:16)

What Is Your Goal?

Reading: Philippians 3:7-21

People in general, including many professing Christians, are more preoccupied with their present and their day-to-day activities than they are with their future—especially when it comes to spiritual things and eternal life. They are satisfied with their general knowledge of Jesus Christ and the routine of "churchgoing" whenever they can. The present seems to be more important and exciting. The present is here and now—the future seems so far away.

Let's not forget that for every today, there was a yesterday and there will be a tomorrow, whether it brings life or death. If it brings death, the ability of the person to determine his or her future is abruptly ended. Death is the door through which a person enters his or her everlasting future.

> *"Then they will go away to eternal punishment, but the righteous to eternal life."* (Matthew 25:46)

Someone who wants to become a doctor must go through studies and training—he cannot make it with just a basic knowledge of the profession. This is a basic principle of life! How, then, can we as Christians be satisfied with just a general knowledge of Christ and a few typical and duty-like spiritual activities—not having a goal or a purpose?

The Apostle Paul wanted to know more about Jesus

Christ and to *"attain to the resurrection of the dead"* (Philippians 3:11). He had a goal, a purpose for living. His goal was eternal life in the Kingdom of God—no matter what the short-term cost was.

In this Bible passage, Paul hasn't reached his goal yet but is on his way. He compares the efforts of a Christian to a marathon or a race. There is a starting point, a track, a goal and, finally, a judge. The runner does not want to be distracted by anything or anyone—his or her eyes are glued to the goal. Neither the past nor other activities must hinder the runner.

> *Therefore, since we are surrounded by such a great cloud of witnesses, let us throw off everything that hinders and the sin that so easily entangles, and let us run with perseverance the race marked out for us.* (Hebrews 12:1)

You cannot run a race unless you know what the goal is—and why you are running. Are you in the race just for the fun of it? Were you forced into it? Or are you just trying to make someone else happy? Maybe you are in the race for the right reasons but are wasting your time running in the wrong direction—not getting any closer to your goal.

The faithful will be rewarded (Daniel 12:3, Ephesians 6:8) and the reward will be eternal (1 Peter 5:4).

> *For our light and momentary troubles are achieving for us an eternal glory that far outweighs them all.* (2 Corinthians 4:17)

Obey or Not Obey?

Reading: Luke 6:46-49

"Why do you call me, 'Lord, Lord,' and do not do what I say?" (Luke 6:46)

A good question, wouldn't you say? The word "Lord" also means "master," doesn't it? If so, then Jesus, as our Lord, must have complete authority over our lives. We belong to Him and must do whatever He says.

That's exactly what you and I are doing, right? Tough question to answer, isn't it? To call Jesus "Lord" and then disobey Him is a contradiction. Only acknowledging Him as Lord is not enough. True love for God and faith in Him require obedience.

The following words are from an engraving from the cathedral of Lubeck, Germany:

> *Thus speaketh Christ our Lord to us,*
> *You call Me master, and obey me not,*
> *You call Me light, and see Me not,*
> *You call Me the way, and walk Me not,*
> *You call Me the life, and live Me not,*
> *You call Me wise, and follow Me not,*
> *You call Me fair, and love Me not,*
> *You call Me rich, and ask Me not,*
> *You call Me eternal, and see me not,*
> *If I condemn thee, blame Me not.*

What aggravated Jesus the most was hypocrisy. Jesus said to the hypocritical religious leaders:

> *Woe to you, teachers of the law and Pharisees, you hypocrites! You clean the outside of the cup and dish, but inside they are full of greed and self-indulgence.* (Matthew 23:25)

To His followers He said,

> *"Not everyone who says to me, 'Lord, Lord,' will enter the kingdom of heaven, but only he who does the will of my Father who is in heaven."* (Matthew 7:21)

To make people understand this very important truth, Jesus told the story of two builders (Matthew 7:24-27).

The wise man is the one who comes to Christ (salvation), hears His words (instruction) and who puts them into practice (obedience). This is the one who builds his life on the principles of Christian discipleship that are found in the Bible. This is the right way to build a life. When the floods and winds of life strike against the house, time after time, the house stands firm because it is built on the rock—Christ and His teachings.

The other man, the foolish one, is the one who hears God's words but does not follow them. He is disobedient. He builds His life on what he thinks is best for him, following worldly principles. When the storms of life rage, his house, which has no foundation, collapses and is swept away, lost forever.

On the Day of Judgment, when people stand before Christ, many will remind Him that they were religious, active members of churches. They will list the miracles they performed and point out that they prophesied or cast out demons—all in His name! But their protests and pleadings will be in vain. Jesus will plainly tell them: *"I never knew you. Away from me, you evildoers!"*

If you hear God's words and do what He says, you will be like the wise man who built his house on the rock. Your life will have a solid foundation and you will not fall when the storms come… because Jesus is the Solid Rock!

"That's All I Want!"

Reading: Psalm 23

A Sunday School child was asked to recite Psalm 23. He stood up with confidence and began: "The Lord is my Shepherd; that's all I want!" It may sound humorous at first, but isn't that exactly what the psalmist meant?

Many people cannot understand how we can claim that Christ is sufficient for all our needs. Is He sufficient only for our religious needs or can He be all we want and need in every area?

Psalm 23 says, *"I shall not be in want."* In other words, "I will be in need of nothing" that Christ cannot provide.

In the Physical Life

"Green pastures" are symbolic of prosperity and provision. He has made us physical creatures and knows our physical needs… and He will supply what we need.

> *"Do not worry about your life, what you will eat or drink; or about your body, what you will wear. Is not life more important than food, and the body more important than clothes?"* (Matthew 6:25)

In the Emotional Life

"Quiet waters" are sadly missing from our frustrated society. The world has never been in greater need of the psychological powers of God and His Word. Troubled consciences, guilt, nervous disorders, fear, anxiety and every disease of the mind can find peace with Him beside the quiet waters.

> *And the peace of God, which transcends all under-*

> *standing, will guard your hearts and your minds in Christ Jesus.* (Philippians 4:7)

IN THE SPIRITUAL LIFE

The soul needs restoration. Originally perfect, created for fellowship with God, man has rejected God and gone his sinful way. Only Christ can change that and make possible the needed reconciliation.

> *Create in me a pure heart, O God, and renew a steadfast spirit within me. Restore to me the joy of your salvation and grant me a willing spirit, to sustain me.* (Psalm 51:10,12)

IN THE MORAL LIFE

"Righteous" means "living in the way that is right; according to God's will" (Nelson Dictionary). That is not easy in today's society where everything and everyone is infected by the terrible disease called "sin". In a world of changing morality, everything is open for change. There must be one unchangeable standard: "He guides me!"

IN THE SOCIAL LIFE

Enemies are inevitable in a person's life. Even Christ had enemies. You don't have to be bad to have enemies! But the Lord, our Shepherd, helps us to properly handle and deal with our enemies.

A successful spiritual life and effective witnessing in today's society are possible only if we are filled with the Holy Spirit, symbolized in Psalm 23 by the anointing of the head with oil.

The need of pleasure and social fellowship is understandable and natural for the physical man. But spiritual fellowship which comes through the new birth brings such a deep joy and pleasure to those who experience it—something unknown to those who are satisfied with the shallow and temporary thrills of worldliness and the flesh. David's joy is clear when he says, *"My cup overflows."*

Satisfaction with life is reflected by the happy Christian who has gratefully received the "goodness and love" which have and will follow him throughout life.

> *For to me, to live is Christ and to die is gain.* (Philippians 1:21)

IN THE CRISIS LIFE

"The valley of the shadow of death" is the price that all men pay for the privilege of life. Life and death go together. When we walk through this shadow and loved ones leave us, His comfort is with us. He walked this way before us and He knows where He is leading us. We must *"fear no evil,"* knowing that He is with us.

> *"Do not let your hearts be troubled. Trust in God; trust also in me.... No one comes to the Father except through me."* (John 14:1,6)

IN THE ETERNAL LIFE

"The house of the Lord" is ready for those whose names are written in the book of life (see Revelation 21:27).

What is heaven to you? Do you believe in heaven? If yes, does heaven mean streets of gold, gates of pearl and walls of jasper? Does it mean reunion with loved ones and rest and joy for eternity?

More than anything else, heaven should mean the place where our Lord is!

> *The city does not need the sun or the moon to shine on it, for the glory of God gives it light, and the Lamb is its lamp.* (Revelation 21:23)

So, all that we need He is and supplies. All other possessions that have not come from Him we neither need nor should have. The Lord our Shepherd knows all our needs… and that's all we need!

The Vanity of Pleasure
Reading: Ecclesiastes 1:12-2:11

From the moment we are born we crave and yearn for pleasure and, as we grow older, that craving grows within us. Everyone searches for and dreams of things that will make them happy—only to find emptiness, disappointment and pain. Lasting joy, happiness and peace in this godless and corrupt world is almost impossible to find.

> *The mirth of the wicked is brief, the joy of the godless lasts but a moment.* (Job 20:5)

If there was such a thing as lasting joy and happiness in the things of the world, the person who should have found it was King Solomon. Solomon had asked God for wisdom but soon found out that:

> *With much wisdom comes much sorrow; the more knowledge, the more grief.* (Ecclesiastes 1:18)

Failing to find fulfillment in intellectual things, Solomon turned to pleasure.

> *I thought in my heart, "Come now, I will test you with pleasure to find out what is good."* (Ecclesiastes 2:1)

Solomon decided that he was going to live it up. He would try to experience every stimulation of the senses known to man. He tried laughter, only to find that behind laughter there is usually sorrow. He turned to wine, but that did not work either. Since wisdom hadn't satisfied him he tried its opposite: folly. Wrong again.

Surely houses and vineyards would make him happier! He built huge parks and gardens with all kinds of fruit trees, reservoirs to water the trees and flowers. He hired thousands of servants and owned the largest herds and flocks. He had the greatest collection of silver and gold. He tried music. He was disappointed again!

He tried sex. He married... not one woman but 700! And, as if these were not enough, he had 300 concubines. But even these 1000 women did not satisfy him. As a matter of fact, his wives led him away from God and to his destruction (1 Kings 11:4-8).

In his search for satisfaction, Solomon had placed no limits and spared no efforts. If he saw something he liked, he bought it. If he thought something would give him pleasure, he did it. Still, when he took an inventory of all that he had done, he found that *"everything was meaningless."* Solomon's search ended in failure.

This does not mean that God is opposed to His people having pleasure.

> *You have made known to me the path of life; you will fill me with joy in your presence, with eternal pleasures at your right hand.* (Psalm 16:11)

Solomon was just looking in the wrong places. He finally discovered that life and its temporary pleasures were meaningless without God.

> *For without him, who can eat or find enjoyment? To the man who pleases him, God gives wisdom, knowledge and happiness.* (Ecclesiastes 2:25-26)

Only Christ can give lasting joy and peace (John 15:11). This complete joy is there for the asking (John 16:24). Where are you searching for your pleasure?

Whose Side Are We On?

Reading: Matthew 16:21-28

When Jesus told His disciples that the time of His death was near, Peter took Him aside and rebuked Him, exclaiming, *"Never, Lord! This shall never happen to you!"* Peter's words were a natural response to something very difficult yet inevitable: death. Even though we know that we will all die, we pretend that it will not happen to us… at least not yet.

Peter loved Jesus very much and could not stand the thought that He was going to die soon. But Jesus had come with a mission: to die for the human race. No one and nothing could have stopped Him from dying. Although Peter's words were meant well, they only succeeded to cause Jesus pain.

Every Christian is called to take up his cross, whatever it may be, and follow our Lord Jesus. However, when that cross appears in the pathway ahead of us, a voice within cries out, "Not now! Get away from me!" or "Why me?" If it is not an inner voice, it may be the voice of a loved one who is trying to deflect us from the path of obedience.

Whatever the cross is, it must be carried even though Satan will try to hinder us. Jesus pointed out to His disciples:

> *"What good will it be for a man if he gains the whole world, yet forfeits his soul?"* (Matthew 16:26)

The meaning is clear: if you are not on God's side, you are a loser. If you are not on God's side, your life is aimless.

What does it mean to be on God's side? How can we get there? For Thomas, that was the crucial question after Jesus had risen from the tomb. He asked, *"Lord, we don't know where you are going; how can we know the way?"* To this Jesus replied:

> *"I am the way and the truth and the life. No one comes to the Father except through me."* (John 14:6)

Jesus has shown us God the Father and the way to Him. Are we on His side? In terms of our relationship with God, we are the ones who are in need of constant change, not God. God is constant, changeless... always on our side.

King David cried out:

> *Where can I go from your Spirit? Where can I flee from your presence? If I go up to the heavens, you are there; if I make my bed in the depths, you are there; if I rise on the wings of the dawn, if I settle on the far side of the sea, even there your hand will guide me.* (Psalm 139:7-10)

If there is one thing we fear more than death, it is the fear of a God who keeps following us, hounding us, calling us to His side. For some people, the real hell of life may not be the thought that they are without God or that there may be no God, but rather, the realization that they cannot get rid of God!

We must remember that, because God loves us so much, He will not leave us alone in death. Whether it is the day-to-day "little" deaths that come to us all, or the death that comes on the last day of our life, our loving Father will not leave us alone. He is with us and for us! But we cannot appreciate that awesome truth and take strength from it unless we are on God's side.

Jesus Reached the Helpless
Reading: John 5:1-15

One of the pictures Jesus saw when He went to Jerusalem was the picture of a society with a great number of suffering people: the blind, sick, lame, paralyzed and leprous. He saw a society so uncaring, so selfish that it abandoned its sick and suffering to the mercy of nature and God. Many of the sick had been brought by family or friends because they had become a burden. They were left there to take care of themselves.

The sad thing in this picture is that even the disabled people did not care about anyone but themselves. Some were able to help themselves, but others were completely helpless. As a matter of fact, one particular man had been waiting there for thirty-eight years for someone to come and help him, but no one had. It seemed no one was interested in him. He had given up all hope; no one was going to help.

But wait a minute! Who was this man coming to him and why was He looking at him in such a compassionate way? The man asked him: *"Do you want to get well?"*

"Do I want to get well? Sir, why do you think I have been waiting here for thirty-eight years? Of course I want to be well, but there is no one to help me."

Jesus, full of compassion, said to him, *"Get up! Pick up your mat and walk."*

This happened 2000 years ago, but the world has not changed much. People are still uncaring and selfish... and today, more than ever before, many are suffering not only physically and emotionally but also, even worse, spiritually. Sadly there still aren't many who are willing to help.

There were three kinds of people in the picture Jesus saw in John 5:1-15: those who had abandoned this man and were too busy doing their own thing, the disabled people who were thinking only of themselves and their own disabilities and the religious people whose main preoccupation was to judge and condemn people.

And then there was JESUS! The compassionate Saviour!

Isn't it the same today? People are spiritually sick and lost. They need Jesus, the Master Healer. They need a friend, someone who cares enough to help them find Jesus. Will you be that friend, that someone?

Prayer

Reading: Matthew 6:5-15

Have you ever wondered how many people who pray actually know whom they are praying to? Do they know why they are praying, or whether their prayers will be heard and answered?

Most religions practise prayer in one form or another. They either pray to one God or to many gods—or even to objects. Followers of these religions often participate in rituals and traditions, not necessarily knowing what they are doing. To encourage their followers to pray, some religions have devised "helps"—prayer books, shawls, beads, rugs and other items.

The Bible says that prayer is speaking with God, the one Living God. Reading or repeating a prayer from a book or making a sign is as logical as a child going to a parent and repeating a memorized statement or making a sign.

Jesus, who did not represent any particular race, religion or man-made doctrine, came to Earth to show us the way and to connect us, the human race, with God the Father.

In Matthew 6:5-9, Jesus said that prayer should be approached sincerely.

> *"When you pray, do not be like the hypocrites, for they love… to be seen by men."* (Matthew 6:5)

If people pray only to impress others then, Jesus declared, the prominence they gain is the only reward they will receive. Jesus went on to say that prayer should not consist of *"empty repetitions"* or babbling (Matthew 6:7). To pray simply because everyone else does it or because we feel obliged to means nothing to God.

To help us better understand prayer, Jesus gave us a model—generally referred to as "The Lord's Prayer", though Jesus didn't necessarily pray it Himself. It was given to His disciples as an example to pattern their own prayers after. This model gives us nine things to remember when praying:

1. We must first acknowledge that God is our Father and sovereign over the universe.
2. We must worship, praise and honour God.
3. We should pray for God's Kingdom on earth when He comes to reign in righteousness.
4. We must acknowledge that God knows what is best for us and surrender our will to His.
5. We should desire that all the heavenly conditions might exist here on earth, too.
6. We can present our own needs, acknowledging our dependence on God for daily food, both spiritual and physical.
7. We must deal with our daily sins and ask for forgiveness in order to restore broken communion with God.

8. We must be willing to forgive others if we expect to be in fellowship with God who has forgiven us.

9. We must acknowledge our total dependence on God for protection from temptation and sin.

Itching Ears
Reading: 2 Timothy 4:1-8

Seeking comfort and avoiding discomfort is a common goal in life. People enjoy pleasant things that stimulate their senses.

No wonder the Apostle Peter warns us:

> *Be on your guard so that you may not be carried away by the error of lawless men and fall from your secure position. But grow in the grace and knowledge of our Lord and Saviour Jesus Christ.* (2 Peter 3:17-18)

Our knowledge of the Lord and Saviour Jesus Christ is based on His declaration:

> *"I am the way and the truth and the life. No one comes to the Father except through me."* (John 14:6)

This truth seems to be objectionable to many "intellectuals" and their concept of justice. Christ made the statement. We can accept it or reject it. The choice is ours—but so is the responsibility of the consequences. We may create our own theologies and philosophies that make us feel more comfortable. We may gather ourselves around theologians and philosophers who tickle our "itching ears".

The increasing interest in sects, cults and the occult, the

attempts to explain the words of the Bible into what human minds may consider to be more "logical", are all signs that the Bible has forewarned us about.

We cannot sit on the fence. We have to make our choice. We can listen to and follow the notions of human wisdom or common sense; or we can accept Christ and follow Him. We can delve into mythology that may please us; or we can search the Scripture. It may not flatter us, but...

> ... *all Scripture is God-breathed and is useful for teaching, rebuking, correcting and training in righteousness, so that the man of God may be thoroughly equipped for every good work.* (2 Timothy 3:16-17)

May the Lord keep us in His grace, and help us to remain faithful servants of His Truth, Jesus Christ our Lord.

It's Easy

Reading: Luke 9:18-27

Advice is easy and cheap, especially when it does not affect us. Almost anything is easy when it does not involve any inconvenience on our part.

It's easy to resist temptation until the temptation is for something you really want to do. Then you begin to find excuses and rationalizations for doing it anyway. Do not be proud that you do not commit the sins for which you condemn another person. He probably is not tempted to commit your favourite sin anymore than you are tempted to commit his.

It's easy to forgive until someone really offends, hurts or does an injustice to you. Then you feel it is okay to strike back, to harbour a grudge or to spread malicious talk about your enemy.

It's easy to be faithful to Christ in worship and study until something else comes along that you really want to do. Then all the old excuses are used: "Only one day to rest", "Such a good day for a picnic", "I won't even be missed", etc.

It's easy to support missionaries and maintain an active program in the local church, especially if you let your financial support stop or go down and let others carry the entire burden.

It's easy to have enough teachers, helpers, and workers if you feel that sort of thing is "their" responsibility and excuse yourself.

It's easy to evangelize and witness for Jesus Christ if it does not interfere with your personal business or professional practice.

It's easy to love others if they will always love you, please you and agree with you.

It's easy to say "I love you" and "You are so wonderful" when someone treats you kindly and pampers you.

It's easy to follow Jesus Christ if there are no real sacrifices and commitments involved.

It's easy to teach and preach about love, holiness, commitment, forgiveness and service as long as you are exempt.

Yes, it's easy to practise cheap, easy "believism". But listen to what Jesus said:

> *"If anyone would come after me, he must deny himself and take up his cross daily and follow me. For whoever wants to save his life will lose it, but whoever loses his life for me will save it."* (Luke 9:23-24)

No, Jesus never said it was going to be easy. But He said He would always be there to help you.

> *"Never will I leave you; never will I forsake you." So we say with confidence, "The Lord is my helper; I will not be afraid."* (Hebrews 13:5-6)

Good Health

Reading: Galatians 5:16-26

Because people have become more health-conscious and concerned about what they eat, more is being said about health and nutrition than ever before. In fact, most of us don't even know what to believe. There are so many conflicting opinions and reports claiming to be the answer to all your health problems and concerns. Even religious organizations and publications have been promoting and selling health products.

Of course, when a Christian organization, magazine or radio station promotes a product, the tendency is to believe that this product's claims must be true. Well, at least for a while, I thought so, too.

There is nothing wrong in caring for our body. As a matter of fact, the Bible says that our bodies are temples of the Holy Spirit, and we have a special obligation to care for them.

> *Do you not know that your body is a temple of the Holy Spirit, who is in you, whom you have received from God?* (1 Corinthians 6:19)

We should get enough rest and proper nourishment, and do everything possible to provide for our physical well-being.

> *A cheerful heart is good medicine.* (Proverbs 17:22)

There is a proven relationship between emotional contentment and good physical health. A happy and cheerful outlook on life has therapeutic value… but that doesn't just happen. True happiness and joy are the result of a right relationship with God and our fellowman. Joy is a result of the Holy Spirit working in our lives.

> *The fruit of the Spirit is love, joy, peace, patience, kindness, goodness, faithfulness, gentleness and self-control.* (Galatians 5:22)

To experience this joy and peace we must live under His control. Real happiness is to know that our sins have been forgiven, that God forgets our sinful past, and that we have been saved and redeemed through personal faith in Jesus Christ. Then, as we walk this journey of life in obedience to His Word, He lights our path and gives us His peace and the joy of His presence.

So, dear reader, be happy. Your spiritual and physical health depends on it.

Pulled in Two Directions

Reading: Philippians 1

Many talk and preach about the beauties of heaven but are busy building empires on earth. Most of us, without hesitation, would say, "I wish our Lord would come right now to take us to our heavenly home." A minute later we would continue planning for our retirement home on earth, forgetting all about heaven.

It's like the person who was asked, "Would you like to go to heaven?" and who answered, "Yes, yes, of course, but not just now. I first have to get married, have a family and then… well, I am sure God understands."

We don't have to feel guilty for having a strong desire to live and enjoy life. Marriage, a family, a fulfilling job, travel, a house—these all have a legitimate appeal. But if the delights of our earthly home are so attractive that we lose sight of God's purpose for putting us here, something is wrong.

As Christians, we are pulled in two directions. We all want to go to heaven, but we want to postpone the journey for as long as we can so we can enjoy the things that give us pleasure here on earth.

The Apostle Paul had mixed feelings, too. Although he desired to be with Christ, he also wanted to live—not just to enjoy life, but because he was needed by the other believers. He said:

> *For to me, to live is Christ and to die is gain… I am torn between the two: I desire to depart and be with Christ, which is better by far; but it is more necessary for you that I remain in the body.* (Philippians 1:21-24)

Paul was pulled in two directions, and in both cases it was for the highest reason.

What about you? If you want to make your stay on earth fruitful and enjoyable, you must keep your eyes on Jesus and heaven in your heart.

True Happiness

Reading: Ecclesiastes 3

There are those who believe and teach that once you are saved and become a follower of Christ, your life changes and you are happy all day. Day after day you are happy.

I don't know about others, but I definitely cannot honestly say that, just because I am a born-again believer and Jesus is my Lord and Saviour, I am happy all day. Sure, I am an optimistic person and when things go wrong I don't despair or panic and let things get me down. But there are times and circumstances when things are certainly not going well and I am not happy or smiling.

You might ask, "Shouldn't our faith in Jesus make us happy all the time? Shouldn't Jesus protect us from all danger and unhappiness? Why does God allow these things to happen to us?"

Well, some people may teach that believers must be happy all the time and have a big smile on, no matter what. But the Bible does not teach that! The Bible makes it very clear that we will have trouble and that we will face tough times. King Solomon said:

> *There is a time to weep and a time to laugh, a time to mourn and a time to dance.* (Ecclesiastes 3:4)

The truth is that Jesus will not protect us from all trouble, but His love and presence will guide us and strengthen us as we go through our struggles.

Instead of trying hard to be happy all day long because we are believers, we must be realistic and say, "No matter what happens, I know that God is in control and He cares for me. And because He who is in me is greater than the one in the world, I can deal with today and, with His help, face tomorrow and whatever it may bring."

You may sometimes see tears in my eyes, but there is peace and joy in my heart. With Jesus Christ, I can have real joy and peace even when things are bad.

Happiness usually depends on happenings and things. Joy depends on Jesus Christ our Lord and Saviour. Are you experiencing His joy and peace?

True Prosperity

Reading: Matthew 7:7-12

"When you become a Christian, your life will change for the better. God will give you prosperity and health. All your problems will be resolved and you won't even have to ask God for things. He will automatically give them to you." I heard a preacher shouting this on the radio one day. He even used some Bible verses to try to support his claim.

Another preacher was challenging people to try God. His message was something like this: "If you give one dollar, God will give you ten dollars. If you give 100 dollars, He will give 1,000 dollars." And so on…

Others preach that a believer does not get sick or, rather, must not be sick because God does not want His children to suffer. People today, more than ever before, seem to be drawn to Jesus by those who proclaim that God wants them healthy and wealthy.

Certainly God cares for the poor and the sick, and surely it is not wrong to pray about our health and other concerns. After all, our heavenly Father cares about us. Jesus said:

> *"Ask and it will be given to you; seek and you will find, knock and the door will be opened to you."* (Matthew 7:7)

But God's greatest concern is not to fill our pockets with money and our houses with wealth. He wants to fill our hearts and lives with love and peace. He wants us to trust Him and obey Him.

When I hear people make promises of wealth and health to those who believe in Jesus, I can't help but wonder if they have ever read these words of Jesus:

> *"If anyone would come after me, he must deny himself and take up his cross and follow me. For whoever wants to save his life will lose it, but whoever loses his life for me will find it. What good will it be for a man if he gains the whole world, yet forfeits his soul? Or what can a man give in exchange for his soul?"* (Matthew 16:24-26)

No, Jesus never promised wealth and prosperity to every believer. And no, He never said that believers will not get sick or lose their jobs or loved ones or go through difficult situations. What Jesus promised was forgiveness, restoration, eternal life and the Holy Spirit who produces the best possible fruit on earth.

> *The fruit of the Spirit is love, joy, peace, patience, kindness, goodness, faithfulness, gentleness and self-control.* (Galatians 5:22)

Is this prosperity or not? Those who have experienced the love of God and are born-again in the family of God are the richest people on earth. Have you experienced Christ's love yet?

When Life Gives You Lemons

Reading: James 1

I was very eager to come to Canada. Many of my friends and my cousin had already left Greece for Canada. I wanted to help my poor parents who were struggling to bring up my sister and me, and the idea of going to Canada excited me.

My parents wrote to my uncle to sponsor me, but the response they received was very disappointing. He would not do it. Sad and broken, I walked out of the house feeling bitter and thinking that life was not fair at all. Not knowing what else to do, I went to downtown Athens and straight to the offices of the Royal Greek Air Force to enlist as a volunteer. I served for twenty-eight months.

Meanwhile, I applied to come to Canada and it took about twenty-four months for my papers to be approved. "Good timing," I thought. I said my goodbyes to my family and friends and came to Canada.

In retrospect, I can see God's hand in this. God had turned the lemon given to me by life into lemonade. I am sure that, at some point in your life, you have felt the same way. Life has a way of giving us lemons instead of the sweet fruit of success.

Your lemon might not have been a serious blow to you; it might have been a brief irritation, like a fender-bender or an out-of-stock item; or it may have been more serious like losing your job, your boyfriend, your money or a loved one. Either way, whether you are ten, twenty or seventy years old, you have learned that life has lemons. The question is, how do we handle these lemons? The book of James deals with that question and uses the word "trials".

James starts by saying that trials may come from God and lead to life:

> *Consider it pure joy, my brothers, whenever you face trials of many kinds, because you know that the testing of your faith develops perseverance.... Blessed is the man who perseveres under trial, because when he has stood the test, he will receive the crown of life that God has promised to those who love Him.* (James 1:2-3,12)

Trials are for our training. We develop spiritual and emotional muscles. But James warns us not to confuse "trials" with "temptations". Temptation comes from us and leads to death.

> *When tempted, no one should say, "God is tempting*

> *me." For God cannot be tempted by evil, nor does he tempt anyone; but each one is tempted when, by his own evil desire, he is dragged away and enticed. Then, after desire has conceived, it gives birth to sin; and sin, when it is full-grown, gives birth to death.* (James 1:13-15)

Because God allows trials to come into our lives to mature us, and because there is a danger that we might blame God for them and complain, or rebel against Him and sin, making a mess of our lives, we must make sure that we respond properly.

The following formula, found in James 1:19, will help us gain the maximum maturity from our troubles. When life gives you a lemon, make lemonade. Here is the recipe for the best lemonade you ever tasted.

BE QUICK TO LISTEN

Who do we need to be quick to listen to? People in general? That, of course, is true and necessary. So much of our conversation is usually centred on our frustrations and personal interests that we are deaf to what others are saying to us.

The context of James 1:19 indicates that he is talking about being quick to hear when you are in the middle of a trial. When trouble comes into our lives, we are slow to hear anyone but ourselves. When our plans are interrupted or we are inconvenienced, we get upset. Then, when anyone tries to tell us something, we are anything but ready to listen. However, James is not exactly talking about listing to others. Being *"quick to listen"* refers to obeying God's Word.

> *Do not merely listen to the word, and so deceive yourselves. Do what it says.* (James 1:22)

The Bible is God's recipe book—if you don't follow the

recipe for making lemonade, you will not have lemonade! When you have a problem, be quick to hear God's Word, obey God's Word and help God's people.

BE SLOW TO SPEAK

Again, this is for the times when we are in trials. If you are talking, you are not listening. If you are not listening, you are not learning. If you are not learning, you are not growing. If you are not growing, you are being overcome instead of overcoming.

To put it plainly, "shut up" and listen to what God is telling you.

BE SLOW TO ANGER

I am amazed at how often, when I counsel people about conflicts or physical or emotional problems, we end up talking about anger. Anger kills you and the person you are angry at.

To sum up, the recipe for lemonade involves actions, words and attitudes. When in the midst of trials, Christians often have the right actions, but their words and attitudes are wrong. Until all three of these areas are right, there will not be spiritual growth and victory over trials.

Get the maximum maturity out of a trial. Make sure your actions, words and attitudes are biblical. Christians must handle their frustrations in a way appropriate to their faith.

Do You Suffer as a Christian?

Reading: 1 Peter 4:12-19

New believers are often surprised by the way their family members, friends and co-workers treat them. They can't understand why people treat them so badly instead of rejoicing with them for the new life and joy they have found in Jesus.

Well, Jesus never said that it was going to be easy to be a Christian. In fact, He taught the very opposite:

> "All men will hate you because of me, but he who stands firm to the end will be saved." (Matthew 10:22)

Trials are to be expected in the life of a Christian. They are tools that perfect us.

REJOICE IN TRIALS

Only a Christian believer can do this! For one thing, when trials come, we are suffering for Christ's sake as He suffered for our sake. The suffering we go through now is nothing in comparison with the glory that we will share at His coming. Furthermore, the Spirit of God rests upon those who are suffering for their faith in Jesus. When the three Hebrew men were thrown in the fiery furnace because of their faith, they believed that God was going to deliver them (Daniel 3:19-30). God not only delivered, but He also walked with them in the fire! We are never alone when we suffer for Christ, for He is with us, giving us the strength we need for every trial.

DO NOT BE ASHAMED OF TRIALS

Roman law required each citizen to pledge loyalty to the Emperor. Once a year, the people would put a pinch of incense on the fire and say, "Caesar is lord!" But the Christian would only confess, "Christ is Lord!" and for that he or she would be arrested, tried and put to death. By bearing Christ's name, Christians were put to shame before their friends. But what a glorious name to bear! It is a name higher than any other name. Why should a believer be ashamed?

Remember that "Christ" means "the anointed one" (in Greek)—the One anointed to save mankind, the Messiah. The children of Israel were expectantly waiting for the Saviour to come. The rest of the world also needed someone who could turn things around, a Saviour. Only God, in His infinite love, could be that Saviour by taking the form of a human in the person of Jesus. He lived among us and eventually died at the age of thirty-three.

Have you made Jesus Christ your Lord and Saviour? Have you ever suffered for doing God's will?

> *So then, those who suffer according to God's will should commit themselves to their faithful Creator and continue to do good.* (1 Peter 4:19)

Life Is Worth Living!
Reading: Ecclesiastes 11:7-12:14

Solomon had already decided that man is not a "cog in the wheel", that there is nothing wrong with enjoying riches and pleasures to God's glory, and that the fact that we do not understand everything about God and life should not be a hindrance to a happy life. Yet Solomon has advice and warning for those who may reject or ignore God and, instead, follow the desires of the flesh.

Note the three key words in the Scripture text given, directed to young and older people alike:

REJOICE

> *Be happy, young man, while you are young, and let your heart give you joy in the days of your youth. Follow the ways of your heart and whatever your eyes see, but know that for all these things God will bring you judgment.* (Ecclesiastes 11:9)

Yes, go ahead and have fun, Solomon said, but unless the fun or joy you get out of doing the things you do are clean, pure and according to God's will, you will have to face judgment. "But what can I do?" you may ask. "I am only responding to my natural desires." Someone might say, "God knows how hard I have tried to stop doing all the things that are bad for me and are against God's will, but I have failed. What can I do?"

REMOVE

> *So then, banish anxiety from your heart and cast off the troubles of your body, for youth and vigour are meaningless.* (Ecclesiastes 11:10)

Spiritual and emotional anxiety is our enemy. Someone may say, "Well, I am too young. I have got to enjoy life now. When I get older I will change." But the wisest man that ever lived says, "No! You are wrong…"

REMEMBER

> *Remember your Creator in the days of your youth, before the days of trouble come and the years approach when you will say, "I find no pleasure in them."* (Ecclesiastes 12:1)

Solomon concludes with these words:

> *Now all has been heard; here is the conclusion of the matter: Fear God and keep His commandments, for this is the whole duty of man. For God will bring every deed into judgment, including every hidden thing, whether it is good or evil.* (Ecclesiastes 12:13-14)

If death really ends all, then life is not worth living—and everything truly is "vanity" and emptiness. But the Bible makes it clear that death is not the end! Because Christ arose from the dead, we shall also be raised! And the glory and reward we enjoy here and in eternity will depend on the life we lived here on earth.

Therefore, let us all live, work and die in the Lord. From man's point of view, it seems like life is futile and empty; all is vanity. But when life is lived in the power of God for the glory of God, then life becomes meaningful.

"If Only"

Reading: Philippians 3:12-16

"If only…" Two small words that say so much. I have heard people say, "If only I had listened," or "If only I had done it differently… but now it's too late."

It was just after I heard someone say, "If only I had done it differently," that I sat down and wrote some "if only" statements I have heard or that people might make:

If only my actions had backed up my words.
If only my many promises had been kept.
If only I had prayed every time I said I would.
If only I had called every time I promised to.
If only I had spent more time with my family.
If only I had studied God's Word more often.
If only I had gone to church more regularly, not just once a week.
If only I had meant it when I said, "I'll be there, Pastor."
If only I had been faithful in following Christ to the end.
If only I had been faithful in serving at church.
If only I had loved God and His Church more than I loved the world.
If only… but that is in the past and is gone. Now it is too late.

Yes, dear reader, it is too late now to change your past. But it is the right time to change your "if onlies" to "I wills" and "I haves". How can you do that? On your own you can't... but God can and will help you do it.

First, bring all your failures and "if onlies" to Christ and leave them there at His feet as an act of confession and surrender. Then ask Him for His forgiveness and restoration. He will respond to you by forgiving you and by giving you a new life to live. Your relationship with Him will be restored and you will have the rest of your life to do the things you should have done but did not.

I hope and pray that there will be no more "if onlies" in your life, but rather, "Praise the Lord" and "Thank you for the privilege, Lord" statements.

Evil Times

Reading: 2 Timothy 3

There is no question that science and technology have come a long way and are advancing rapidly. In the past, it took weeks or months to send a message across the Atlantic Ocean. Several years ago we were fascinated by the fax machine, which did the job in minutes. Now, with the growth of Internet and e-mail use, messages are transmitted faster than you can blink.

Man has always pursued knowledge and ways to improve his life. Unfortunately, this basic desire seems to have become an obsession. Man wants to discover more, invent more, build better tools and machinery, produce better and faster transportation, construct bigger and taller buildings...

You'd think that this pursuit of perfection would have made this world a better place to live and made man a better person to live with. On the contrary, our world is almost completely ruined! Instead of water and food supplies increasing, people everywhere are dying of hunger and thirst. Also, man and woman's character continues to deteriorate.

No one should be surprised about this reality that was predicted 2000 years ago by the Apostle Paul.

> *But mark this: There will be terrible times in the last days.* (2 Timothy 3:1)

Although we cannot predict the exact time of the "end", we can see its signs around us as pointed out in the Word of God. We are told that people will reject God and follow their own selfish desires; sin will increase to the point of making life on earth unbearable. Even nature and the animal world will be affected.

We see these signs in the newspapers and on television: crime, broken families, air and water pollution, and fatal diseases. Even the way the world makes fun of Christians was predicted.

> *First of all, you must understand that in the last days scoffers will come, scoffing and following their own evil desires. They will say, "Where is this 'coming' he promised? Ever since our fathers died, everything goes on as it has since the beginning of creation."* (2 Peter 3:3-4)

In 2 Timothy 3:5 we are told about a "form of godliness" without life-changing power. This world is full of religion… but without God's power it is useless, even dangerous! Paul tells us to keep away from godless religion.

Do you yearn to live a godly life? With God's help, follow Paul's advice:

> *In fact, everyone who wants to live a godly life in Christ Jesus will be persecuted, while evil men and impostors will*

go from bad to worse, deceiving and being deceived. But as for you, continue in what you have learned and have become convinced of, because you know those from whom you learned it, and how from infancy you have known the holy Scriptures, which are able to make you wise for salvation through faith in Christ Jesus. (2 Timothy 3:12-15)

Let Us Go On

Reading: Hebrews 6:1-12

The world situation has most people worried. It is rare to hear a news report that isn't about a revolution, a war, a murder, a suicide or corruption among those in high places. No country seems to be immune from this moral and spiritual disintegration.

It can be discouraging and distressing to think about the future but, whatever happens, we must keep going on! We cannot turn back. Whatever the path before us, we must walk it. Time is like a policeman that says, "Keep moving."

As we go, we must look out for the signs and warnings along the way. The side roads are plainly marked: Misery, Ruin and Death. The right path is also clearly shown: Blessing, Peace, Eternal Life and Heaven. We must keep going, but we have to be sure that we are on the right path—the straight and narrow way.

> *"Enter through the narrow gate. For wide is the gate and broad is the road that leads to destruction, and many enter through it. But small is the gate and narrow the road that leads to life, and only a few find it." (Matthew 7:13-14)*

Although pressed for time, we must proceed carefully and

slowly. It is better not to slip than to have to get up after a fall (although, of course, it is better to get up after a fall than to stay down!) There are "yellow lights" of caution, "red lights" warning of danger and "green lights" of safety. Throughout the year, we must keep the lamp of the Word of God—our green light—high as a light for our feet.

Let's not go alone, though. Let us look for friends on the way. Let us also look out for those that need our help. In any case, we are never alone if we are walking with Jesus every day, all the way. Look forward with hope to the end of the way. Christ promises help and comfort. A holy way is a happy way.

So, how do you get to heaven? Take the first turn to the right and then keep straight ahead.

Disappointed and Disillusioned?

Reading: Psalm 71

When things do not go the way we had hoped, we are very often disappointed and, if other people have caused part of this disappointment, we go deeper into disillusionment.

The disappointments of this world, however, are only temporary and we must think of them as such and strengthen ourselves to be able to cope with them. Spiritual strength will help us deal with our disappointments.

> *For our light and momentary troubles are achieving for us an eternal glory that far outweighs them all. So we fix our eyes not on what is seen, but on what is unseen. For what is seen is temporary, but what is unseen is eternal.*
> (2 Corinthians 4:17-18)

When disappointed and discouraged, with no one to turn to, just remember the One who never disappoints. You can always turn to your only Hope (see Psalm 130:1-6). We should also know that some of the disappointments and disillusionments we go through may be the Lord's way of testing us or preparing us for the future and for what might be ahead.

Very often we feel let down, unjustly treated, ignored. "Why do others have so much more than I have, even though I work so hard? Why didn't I get that promotion?" After a while, these feelings turn into bitterness and make it even more difficult to cope with our problems.

Let us not forget that all things come to all people and today's disappointment may be shared by someone else tomorrow. When we are happy, do we wonder why others are not as happy as we are (see Proverbs 10:3,6-9; Ecclesiastes 9:11-16)?

It is important to understand that, at all times, our disappointments are with men, never with God or with Jesus. If we realize this, we will know for certain that we are never alone. All we have to do is ask for comfort from the Comforter.

> *Your righteousness reaches to the skies, O God, you who have done great things. Who, O God, is like you? Though you have made me see troubles, many and bitter, you will restore my life again; from the depths of the earth you will again bring me up. You will increase my honor and comfort me once again.* (Psalm 71:19-21)

Very often we let ourselves become disillusioned, forgetting the example of our Lord Jesus Christ who, while knowing He would be betrayed, never stopped serving and loving mankind so freely (see Matthew 17:22,24; 26:1-4). If Jesus could accept Peter's denial even though he was so close to Him, surely we must be able to face everything that comes our way (see Matthew 26:34-36,69-75).

Let us remember that we are not the first nor the last ones to be disappointed and disillusioned but, as Daniel was comforted, we will also be comforted.

Additional reading: Daniel 10:18-19; 12:2-3; Psalm 23:4; 2 Corinthians 1:3-4; Acts 9:31

Anxiety and Worry
Reading: Psalm 42

Do you ever worry? Are you concerned about your job, your family and your future? Have you ever felt so anxious that you could not eat, sleep or work? Did you ever go to the doctor or hospital thinking that you are having a heart attack, only to be told that everything is fine and that it is only anxiety you are suffering from?

When you returned home you might have started thinking about these anxiety attacks and what causes them. Not knowing the causes can make you sink deeper into anxiety and depression. People may start asking you all kinds of questions about the reasons for your condition, not realizing that, rather than helping you, they are making a bad situation even worse.

If you have experienced or are going through a situation like this, you know how difficult it can be for you and for those around you.

Worrying seems to be part of our nature and the pressures of our modern world have aggravated the problem. The sad thing is that those who are anxious and worry too much are so preoccupied with what may happen in the future that they forget or are unable to cope with the present.

There are many who are anxious about imagined shortcomings, about the future, their health, their families and their work. If no one has been able to understand you and your situation and you are about to give up and settle into depression, please don't. Bring all your worries and anxiety to Jesus Christ who not only understands you but is also ready to help you.

> *Cast all your anxiety on him, because he cares for you.* (1 Peter 5:7)

When the writer of Psalm 42 was depressed, he had this conversation with himself:

> *Why are you downcast, O my Soul? Why so disturbed within me? Put your hope in God, for I will yet praise Him My Saviour and my God.* (Psalm 42:5)

Have you put your hope in God?

Direct Prayer Line

Reading: Psalm 34

Imagine there is an emergency and you want to call someone you know for help. You quickly dial the number, hoping the person is there. To your frustration, after a short busy signal, you hear the following message: "Let Bell notify you if this line becomes free in the next thirty minutes. Press star. A seventy-five-cent charge applies."

Frustrated, you press the star button, hang up and wait. Half an hour goes by and still nothing. You dial again and the same annoying message is played. You really need to reach this person, but you can't. You hang up and, in desperation, you want to cry.

You know what you go through sometimes, trying to reach someone for help or just to talk to. You often end up getting a pre-recorded message or having to leave a message with the hopes that someone will listen to it and respond. It seems like there are no direct lines. You have to go through complicated machinery and a time-consuming process to reach someone you need to contact.

But the wonderful news is that there is a direct, toll-free line to God for immediate access. You don't get a busy signal, you don't have to go through an operator or a very complicated voice mail system, nor are you ever put on hold. Your call reaches God immediately.

There is no delay or interruption, no need for intermediary, no need to compose a perfect prayer, no need to even utter any words. He can hear your broken heart, see your tears and read your mind. All you have to do is dial the toll-free number.

King David said:

> *The eyes of the LORD are on the righteous, and His ears are open to their cry.* (Psalm 34:15)

and...

> *I lay my requests before you and wait in expectation.* (Psalm 5:3)

Not only can God be reached at any time, but what is also wonderful is that you can stay on the line all day. One of the shortest verses says:

> *Pray continually.* (1 Thessalonians 5:17)

What a wonderful Creator, what a loving Father and what a privilege to be able to speak to Him at any time, from any place, about anything... and know that He hears us!

Dear reader, are you making good use of your direct line to God?

Joy and Peace
Reading: Romans 5:1-11

"Buy this phone and get your life back!" "Look good, feel better. The sooner you get started, the sooner you will achieve your personal best! Buy our video!" "If you haven't unravelled the meaning of life—all you have to do is watch Life Network television."

These advertisements were found in the women's magazine *Chatelaine* and are only a small sample of the millions of ads that are seen and heard everyday.

No matter who or where you are, in one way or another, you are exposed to advertisements, sales pitches, promises and gimmicks of all kinds—some direct and others indirect. They promise more joy and happiness, more leisure time (which of course brings more joy) or a new way of life full of joy... if, of course, you buy their product, join their club or support their organization.

These influences are present, not only in the commercial world, but in the religious world as well. Countless religious groups and organizations are eager to sell you their products, ideas, methods, books, etc. And the competition is fierce. The world has rediscovered (or, rather, the devil has reintroduced) the goddess of pleasure and sensuality. Satan has done so by repackaging the old product of "sensual and sinful passions" and renaming it "joy and happiness".

Pleasure, especially of the physical kind, seems to be the ultimate goal for most people today. Instead of asking, "Is this true?" they ask, "Is this physically or spiritually pleasing?" Often people join a religion, not because they have found the truth or to worship God, but because of the pleasure they hope to get.

There is nothing wrong with getting pleasure out of worshipping God—that's how it should be. But it becomes a problem when that pleasure becomes the purpose for worshipping God. A spiritual high is short-lived if it is simply the result of a beautiful melody or prayer—unless that song or prayer is first a result of knowing and worshipping God.

When people try to sell you joy, be sure to read the fine print. Look for the source of that happiness. Jesus is not a salesman of pleasure—He is the Giver of peace, joy and happiness. He said:

> *"Peace I leave with you; my peace I give you. I do not give to you as the world gives. Do not let your hearts be troubled and do not be afraid."* (John 14:27)

True joy is found only in God.

> *You have made known to me the path of life; you will fill me with joy in your presence, with eternal pleasures at your right hand.* (Psalm 16:11)

True joy is the result of salvation.

> *With joy you will draw water from the wells of salvation.* (Isaiah 12:3)

The joy that comes from God through Christ is complete.

> *"Until now you have not asked for anything in my name. Ask and you will receive, and your joy will be complete."* (John 16:24)

The joy of the Lord is perfect. It is not a continuous state of painlessness or freedom from problems, but it is a real and lasting awareness of God's presence and love in our daily lives.

Have you experienced God's joy yet?

Why Do I Keep Stumbling?

Reading: 2 Peter 1:3-10

"No matter how hard I try, I keep stumbling and falling in my spiritual walk. Why? What is the problem? What is missing in my Christian living? I have tried all kinds of recipes, but nothing seems to work." That's how a young lady expressed her frustration to me one day.

Well, stumbling seems to be inevitable and, unless we watch each step we take, we will stumble and fall. But the Bible does give us the recipe for effective Christian living. The two main ingredients God provides are:

HIS DIVINE POWER

> *His divine power has given us everything we need for life and godliness through our knowledge of Him.* (2 Peter 1:3)

HIS PRECIOUS PROMISES

> *Through these he has given us his very great and precious promises, so that through them you may participate in the divine nature and escape the corruption in the world caused by evil desires.* (2 Peter 1:4)

As we thoroughly blend His power and promises into our daily believing and living, we will be more like Christ our Lord. But it is very important to add the following ingredients to our faith: virtue, knowledge, self-control, perseverance, godliness, brotherly kindness and love. If we include each of these, we will be fruitful and we will not stumble in our walk with the Lord. Anyone who neglects these vital ingredients is short-sighted, even blind, and has forgotten that he was cleansed from his old sins.

Dear reader, don't change God's ingredients and then blame Him and His recipe when things go wrong. Instead, follow His instructions carefully and faithfully. God's recipe brings spiritual success.

Holiness
Reading: 1 Peter 1:13-25

People are looking for miracles today, perhaps more than ever before. Even those who don't believe in God or practise any religion look for miracles, especially when everything else seems to have failed. Some religious people—particularly Christians—often become obsessed with the need to experience or witness miracles.

I strongly believe in miracles and that, even today, God is at work healing, mending and transforming lives. However, when miracles become the main preoccupation of believers and churches and when, instead of asking for God's mercy and for His will to be done, they demand a miracle of healing, I am afraid they are neglecting to see the greatest miracle of all: holiness.

When God takes an unholy person out of an unholy world, makes that person holy, puts him back into the unholy world and then keeps him holy, that is the greatest miracle that God can do today. No matter who the person is, he can experience this miracle if he is willing to invite Christ into his life, make Him his Lord and then walk in holiness.

But just as He who called you is holy, so be holy in all

you do; for it is written: "Be holy, because I am holy." (1 Peter 1:15-16)

When holiness is neglected, Christians lose their ability to recognize and deal with sin. But when you allow the Holy Spirit's purifying flame to burn brightly in your life, He will increase your sensitivity to sin and your ability to discern right from wrong.

The words *"be holy"* are not words to be repeated only when we teach or preach. They are a serious commandment from our Lord who died on the cross for our redemption. Many believers forget that the true Christian ideal is not to be happy, but to be holy. The Holy Spirit can only dwell in a holy heart.

If you are filled with the presence of the Holy Spirit and are patterning your daily conduct according to His will, then you will enjoy His empowering presence and the joy that comes to all who aim for holiness.

Are You without Sin?

Reading: John 8:1-11

Jesus went to the temple to teach one day. He had a message for the people who cared to come and listen to Him—a message of hope, forgiveness and life.

Many came to hear Jesus, this teacher who had captivated people's hearts with His simple yet effective way of teaching, healing and loving the sinners and the broken-hearted. However, some self-righteous religious leaders came to criticize and condemn Jesus. These people had not come to learn from Jesus but, they thought, to teach Him a lesson.

There are people today who go from church to church looking for one that is to their liking, leaving one church after the other, finding fault with something or someone and throwing a couple of stones as if they have no faults of their own.

The teachers and Pharisees did this when they brought in a woman caught in adultery, ready to stone her. They conveniently forgot to bring the man with whom she was caught and they adjusted the law to cover up their hypocrisy. The law required the execution of both parties—not only the woman—as we see in Leviticus 20:10.

But Jesus had come to mend and save lives, not to destroy them. He looked at this despised, lost and sinful woman and saw a precious soul, ready to be saved, cleansed, restored and made useful. The religious leaders had condemned her and were ready to kill her, but Jesus loved her and saved her from physical and spiritual death.

When Jesus forgave her, no one there was able to condemn her. When Jesus saves us, we are justified and made whole and holy, just as if we had never sinned.

Jesus said to the woman,

"Go now and leave your life of sin." (John 8:11)

He was telling her that he forgave her past, no matter how terrible it was, but, from then on, she was not to return to her old sinful way of life.

No matter who you are and how often you have been judged and condemned by people, Jesus is ready to forgive you, to mend and restore your life and to give you peace.

Do you need His forgiveness and peace? If yes, please ask Him for it now. He will not reject or ignore you. He is ready to give you a new start, a new life, if you ask Him.

Be Clean

Reading: Matthew 7:28-8:4

Jesus' famous Sermon on the Mount was a call to moral and ethical living and was, no doubt, meant to give Christians a standard to follow. Today, however, there seem to be no more moral and ethical standards.

> *When Jesus had finished saying these things, the crowds were amazed at his teaching, because he taught as one who had authority, and not as their teachers of the law.* (Matthew 7:28-29)

Jesus' powerful words and deeds astonished people. He had come to minister, not to be ministered to.

The multitudes that had followed Him saw something unusual: a leper kneeling before Jesus instead of running away from the crowd.

THE LEPER AND THE CROWD

This crowd was in no mood for lepers. Lepers were outcasts and no one would go near them. They had just heard a beautiful sermon and were on a spiritual high, perhaps. They were happy. Now this leper would spoil it all!

But good sermons are not meant to merely make us feel good and self-righteous. Often they are meant to prepare us to care for and serve others.

The lepers in the Bible give us a good picture of what sin has done to all of us: we are all unclean.

> *There is no one righteous, not even one; there is no one*

who understands, no one who seeks God. All have turned away, they have together become worthless; there is no one who does good, not even one. (Romans 3:10-12)

Our sins have earned us death.

For the wages of sin is death but the gift of God is eternal life in Christ Jesus our Lord. (Romans 6:23)

Sadly, many Christians have no time or compassion for the "unclean". They want Jesus to save only clean and respectable people... but Jesus came to save the unclean and the lost!

"For the Son of Man came to seek and to save what was lost." (Luke 19:10)

The Leper and Christ

The leper came and worshipped Jesus and called Him Lord... just like the thief on the cross (Luke 23:42) and the woman caught in adultery (Luke 8:11) did. This leper actually believed that Jesus could do anything—even heal him.

Jesus was full of compassion for this man (Mark 1:41). Compassion is feeling what another feels—not just saying that you do. Jesus could identify with the man's pain.

Jesus touched the rejected then and still touches those who need Him today. Do we touch anyone in the name of Jesus? Or are we ignoring the untouchables? Yes, God touches people today... but He uses people like you and me.

The Leper Made Clean

Jesus said to the leper: "I am willing, be clean!" Jesus wants to make people clean and no one is too dirty for Jesus to clean. Imagine this leper's joy at being healed. Have you experienced the joy of being made clean?

Additional reading: 1 John 1:7-9

Cut It Off!

Reading: Mark 9:42-50

When my mother was seven years old she was working as a servant girl. Somehow she developed a sore just above her right ankle. With her family's situation and the lack of medical facilities, her leg could not be treated and the sore became gangrene, eventually leading to the amputation of her leg just below the knee.

At that early age, my mother's leg was cut off to save her life. Amputation is a drastic way of fighting disease, but there are times when nothing less will preserve a life. If you were given a choice between your leg and your life, I am sure you would rather give up a leg than your life.

Sin is a disease that destroys the human soul. Jesus knew how destructive sin could be so He recommended and even encouraged spiritual "amputation"— cutting off sin.

What are the consequences of continuing in sin? If we are ruled by sin, we will surely be ruined and destroyed by it. The problem is that we are not often horrified by sin—or even bothered by it! We allow sin to creep into our lives and drain us from the vitality and joy that Jesus has given to us. We don't realize that every sin that we do not deal with makes us weaker and less effective in fighting sin. Sin is like a sore that develops into gangrene because we refuse to have it cleaned out and treated.

Not being willing to give up a sin because we enjoy it so much and because it looks so small and innocent is like someone who will not let his foot be amputated—even though he is warned that the gangrene will kill him—because he loves playing hockey.

If you think that giving up sin is hard and unfair, just remember what Jesus says in Mark 9:42-50. Using the hand, foot and eye as examples, He explains that it is better to lose that body part and to live than to hold on to something that is rotting your life away, both spiritually and physically.

I know that giving up things that we enjoy is neither natural nor easy but, with God's help, we must do it if we want to live peaceful and godly lives without guilt or turmoil. Confession and abandonment of sin is the only way.

I invite you to pray the following prayer:

> *Father, I confess that sin does not always horrify me as it should. Too often I allow sin to stay in my life and drain me of the joy You have given me. I acknowledge that every sin that I do not deal with makes me weaker and less effective for You. Make me willing, Father, to take radical action against sin. And Lord, thank You for the power to conquer sin through Jesus Christ.*

Christ or Satan?

Reading: 2 Corinthians 6:14-7:1

The problems in the church of Corinth were spiritual ones: the people were not living like Christians; they were compromising with sin.

It is a basic principle of life that opposites cannot fellowship together. These Corinthians were yoking themselves with unbelievers in marriage, in social life, in business and in other ways. They were losing their testimonies for Christ. After all, if a Christian lives like the rest of the world, how can he witness to the world?

Let's look at opposites mentioned in this passage of Scripture: righteousness and wickedness, light and darkness, Christ and Belial (Satan), believer and unbeliever, temple of God and idols.

The attitude of too many Christians today is that the Church should compromise and please the world in order to "win" the world. As a result, the compromising Christian gets a compromising church. But the Bible makes it very clear that there must be separation from sin. This does not mean isolating from or leaving the world. It means keeping ourselves from the sinful things of the world. Separation... not integration or compromise.

Paul asks the question:

> *What does a believer have in common with an unbeliever?... What agreement is there between the Temple of God and idols? For we are the Temple of the living God.* (2 Corinthians 6:15-16)

The obvious question, then, is "Why do so many Christians compromise with the things of the world?" Why, for example, will they get involved in the occult even though the Bible forbids it? Is it because they don't understand the Bible? Is it to get the things that God will not give them? Or is it because they don't know that,

> *... the one who is in [them] is greater than the one who is in the world.* (1 John 4:4)

If Christ is greater than Satan, the prince of this world, why do we need fortune tellers or a horoscope to tell us about our future, which is in God's hands? How dare we consult the devil about things that are God's business?

> *What harmony is there between Christ and Satan?* (2 Corinthians 6:15)

Another tool the devil successfully uses, not only in the

world, but in many churches, too, is rock music. Unfortunately, many churches and believers listen to it, use it and are hooked on it... not knowing that they are helping the devil with his destructive work.

We don't need Satan's help to live happy and fulfilled lives. We don't need to go to him or his angels of darkness for pleasure. The only things Satan has to offer are lies, pain, disappointment, loneliness and death. God is all we need. He is all-sufficient.

> *Let us purify ourselves from everything that contaminates body and spirit, perfecting holiness out of reverence for God.* (2 Corinthians 7:1)

"We Don't Need More Entertainment"

Reading: Acts 19

Many people have the impression that by lowering the standards of the Christian faith and the gospel to those of the world, they will be able to effectively reach the world and make it easy for people to accept Christ and become Christians.

They actually think the closer you bring Christianity to the world, the more likely it is that the world will accept the gospel of Jesus Christ. They are convinced that by not talking about things like sin, judgment, hell and holiness people will be willing to join the Church. Anything that might sound harsh or politically not so correct is not mentioned or is explained to mean something else.

What these Christians don't realize is that people are sick and tired of the empty promises and lies this godless world offers. If people did not want to change their way of life and be bothered by God's standards and by heaven and hell, why would they ever want to join a church or follow a religion that is no different than what they now have anyway?

Not long ago at a meeting with church leaders and ministers, while I was commenting about the need for holiness and a disciplined life and the necessity to teach our youth about holiness, I was stopped and told that I had it all wrong. "The youth today need more entertainment and activities—not talks about holiness. And if you can't understand that, then your church will lose its youth," I was told.

Well, I knew what the Bible says but, just the same, the following day I asked some of our young people at church whether they wanted more entertainment and activities or to continue with our Bible studies and equipping classes of evangelism and holy living.

Their answer was: "Pastor, if we wanted more entertainment and fun we would have stayed in the world. There is a lot more entertainment there than in the Church. We want more than what the world offers."

In the Book of Acts, the lives of the true believers were so different that others began to call them Christians (Acts 11:26). In the New Testament, Christians were referred to as "saints" (set apart ones).

Nothing preaches louder than a holy life—unless it is an unholy life. Then the message is drowned out by the sinful life of the messenger.

In Acts 19, the believers took their Christianity seriously. They confessed deeds that had no place in their lives, destroyed books that had no place on their shelves and developed a convicting testimony for the Lord.

Is there something in your life that you must deal with? As you stand before God today, ask the Holy Spirit to reveal any object, idea or relationship from your past that may be hindering your spiritual growth. Ask Him to show you how you, too, like the believers in Acts 19, can have it removed from your life.

Avoid the Fruitless Deeds of Darkness

Reading: Ephesians 5:1-21

I am sure you have heard the saying, "Tell me who your friends are and I will tell you who you are."
The Bible makes it very clear that true believers should

> ... *have nothing to do with the fruitless deeds of darkness, but rather expose them.* (Ephesians 5:11)

Remember: bad company corrupts good morals. Where good and evil are found together, trouble will follow. The believer is called not only to abstain from the unfruitful works of darkness, but also to expose them.

The believer does this in two ways. First, by a life of holiness and, second, by words of correction spoken under the direction of the Holy Spirit. The follower of Christ who is filled with the Holy Spirit must not be part of any moral corruption, but rather must rebuke it.

It is so sad to see so many who call themselves Christians not only participating in unnatural forms of sin and feeling very comfortable talking about them, but also influencing others in the Church. To make things worse, many churches, either because they want to be politically correct or because they have lowered their biblical moral standards, have compromised and allowed sin into the Church, even though God says, *"Have nothing to do with the works of darkness."*

Light exposes whatever is in darkness. Likewise, a holy Christian life reveals by contrast the sinfulness of sinful lives. Of course, those who have grown accustomed to the dark shy away from the light because they do not want their wickedness to be exposed.

The life of the believer should always be like a sermon, exposing darkness. Your task, dear reader, as the light of the world, is to remove yourself from the darkness that has surrounded you and expose the deeds of darkness there. Only then will you

> *… become blameless and pure, [child] of God, without fault in a crooked and depraved generation, in which you shine like stars in the universe.* (Philippians 2:15)

You will be an influence for goodness and holiness—rather than a casualty.

The Sin of the Heart
Reading: Colossians 3:1-17

Although Jesus condemned all sin and sinfulness, it was the sins of the heart—not of the flesh—that He spoke the harshest against. Why? Ultimately, the seat of all evil is the centre of our inmost motives and intentions. Pride, envy, self-centredness, lack of love and hypocrisy are the real monsters.

It is the "lie in the soul" that must be attacked more than anything else. The source of the infection must be attacked and removed to prevent the spreading of the disease and death. If you want to remove a bad tree because it is damaging the foundation of your house, you attack and remove the roots... not the fruit or the leaves.

This is where many Christians tend to compromise the most, excusing and tolerating sin and divisiveness within the Church fellowship. Sins like racial discrimination, jealousy, envy, lust of power, sexual immorality and lack of holiness do not seem to be recognized as a real danger to the Church today.

Jesus was very clear when He condemned these sins, but it seems that we do not consider them serious enough to require repentance, a change of our ways and holiness. It is sad to hear Christians excuse this condition and explain it away as natural and inevitable, claiming that this is how we were made. This is not, however, the mind that was in Jesus Christ, and it is His mind we need to have.

> *For who has known the mind of the Lord that He may instruct him? But we have the mind of Christ.* (1 Corinthians 2:16)
>
> *Your attitude should be the same as that of Christ Jesus....* (Philippians 2:5)
>
> *Set your minds on things above, not on earthly things.* (Colossians 3:2)

It should be our desire and the desire of the Church to live consistently in a spirit of holiness. Each of us must discipline himself or herself, remembering that sin begins in the heart.

Are you willing to have your heart examined by the Holy Spirit? If there are things that must go, are you willing to let the Holy Spirit purify your heart?

Sin Is Sin
(no matter what you call it)

Reading: Isaiah 5:8-30

A church leader stormed into his pastor's study and insisted that the minister stop preaching so plainly about sin. He said that the young people of the church would be tempted to try it for themselves, if they heard so much about it. He went on to suggest that the pastor should simply refer to these sins as "mistakes" and go no further.

The wise pastor quickly went to one of his closets where he kept some cleaning material and took out a bottle. Returning to the church leader who was still upset, he said, "I see what you mean." Showing him the bottle marked with big letters, POISON, he said: "Suppose I remove this label and put one on that reads 'antacid'... will that be good?"

"Don't you see?" the pastor continued. "The milder you make the label, the more deadly you make the poison!"

Sin is sin... no matter what you call it or what label you put on it! God hates sin. It is the most deadly poison. It kills the soul if it is not confessed and removed from the life of the believer.

Every preacher, teacher and church leader must warn people about the dangerous consequences of sin. Listen to what God asked Isaiah to do. God said:

> *Shout it aloud, do not hold back. Raise your voice like trumpet. Declare to my people their rebellion and... their sins.* (Isaiah 58:1)

Why is it that many trumpeters who have been commissioned are silent? Have the warning labels been replaced with less threatening labels?

I am afraid so. Most sins are now labelled "lifestyle", "error", "mistake" or "fine, as long as you don't harm anyone." But the Bible still calls them "sin" and marks them: "Danger! Don't touch!"

> *Woe to those who call evil good and good evil, who put darkness for light and light for darkness, who call bitter for sweet and sweet for bitter.* (Isaiah 5:20)

Salvation involves turning away from sin, not only changing the labels!

If you are a Christian but have not been living a life that pleases Christ, if sin has robbed you of blessings and joy and if you honestly want to quit sinning and live a life of holiness, confess your unconfessed sins to God and ask for forgiveness. Then trust Jesus Christ as your Lord and Saviour.

> *Everyone who calls on the name of the Lord will be saved.* (Romans 10:13)

Have you made peace with God?

No One Understands Like Jesus

Reading: Psalm 8

No one understands! No one even wants to understand! At least it seems that way sometimes, doesn't it? You have hurts, needs, longings, and no one seems to know or care. And so you go on hurting, not knowing why you are being ignored.

But, how could they know? People may be all around you, but they can't look inside you to see what you really are, how you feel or why you do what you do.

Ever since creation men and women have felt that way. They have been reaching out for something or someone to understand, to help them face the basic issues of life, and, sadly, they have come to the conclusion that no one understands them or cares. So they have locked themselves into a private prison or have walked away from God.

But there are also many who have discovered that, while they were searching, someone was reaching out to them, ready to help. God is always reaching out to help either directly or indirectly through others. It's true that people may not always understand or care for you, but your Creator and Sustainer does!

Listen to what King David said:

> *What is man that you are mindful of him, the son of man that you care for him?* (Psalm 8:4)

Jesus said:

> *"My command is this: Love each other as I have loved you. Greater love has no one than this, that he lay down his life for his friends. You are my friends if you do what I command."* (John 15:12-14)

Dear reader, remember this: It is because no one understands like Jesus that He came to this earth. God Himself came in the flesh to suffer and die for our salvation. The Prophet Isaiah said:

> *Surely He took up our infirmities and carried our sorrows.* (Isaiah 53:4)

Could there have been a more sacrificial way of reaching out to all humanity, to you and me?

The good news is that our Saviour is not dead. He is alive and interceding for us. Yes, Jesus understands and cares and He is always ready to help.

John W. Peterson's well-known hymn, "No One Understands like Jesus", expresses this truth so well:

No one understands like Jesus, He's a friend beyond compare.
Meet Him at the throne of mercy, He is waiting for you there.
No one understand like Jesus, when the days are dark and grim;
No one is so near, so dear as Jesus. Cast every care on Him.

Love—the Most Effective Tool
Reading: 1 Corinthians 13

Isn't it wonderful that the powerful force behind the gospel of Jesus Christ is love? The most important element in the building of Christ's Church is very simply love—something we often take for granted.

Love is the essence of God's nature, the perfection of human character and the ultimate power in the universe. Love is also the Church's most powerful tool. Unfortunately, we sometimes don't possess, let alone use, this effective instrument. Christians ask God for all kinds of great gifts but neglect love. Spiritual gifts are wonderful, but love is the greatest of all gifts.

Churches that seek supernatural experiences more than Christian holiness and growth very often end up divided, confused and carnal. The church of Corinth had this problem. The Apostle Paul deals with the question of spiritual gifts in 1 Corinthians 12 because this was their main preoccupation. He closes the chapter with these words:

> *And now I will show you the most excellent way.*
> (1 Corinthians 12:31)

Paul then devotes a whole chapter to teaching about love. He made three main points.

LOVE IS ESSENTIAL

Many people desire the gift of preaching or teaching, both of which are good. However, the Bible points out that even if one could speak like an angel, if he had no love, he would be a useless sound. Preaching without love is just making a noise. Praying without love is just empty speech. Giving without love is just a ceremony.

Jesus asked Peter three times if he loved Him (John 21:17). Although Peter had given up everything for Jesus, it was his love that was required more than anything else.

LOVE IS EFFECTIVE

Love is patient and kind; it doesn't burn with jealousy. Envy is a terrible sin! Love is not boastful or proud. It isn't rude or self-seeking. It is forgiving—in other words, it doesn't remember wrongs. Love doesn't delight in seeing others suffer. It always protects, trusts, hopes and perseveres.

If you can replace the word "love" in the phrases above with your name and end up with a truthful statement about yourself, then you are effective as a Christian. You are "successful" in reaching others with the love of God.

LOVE IS ETERNAL

Love never fails. The original Greek says that love will never stop existing—unlike all the other gifts. Why? Because God is love and God is eternal!

Let's ask God to give us the ability to love. As Paul said to the Corinthians, *"Let us follow the way of love"* (1 Corinthians 14:1).

Honouring Mothers

Reading: Proverbs 31

Not everyone becomes a mother, but everyone has a mother! Each year on Mother's Day, most of us take some time to remember, honour and send a card or flowers to our mothers.

It would be ridiculous to suggest that we honour our mothers only once a year on Mother's Day, but I wonder how often we actually do stop to appreciate them.

The Bible says,

> *Honor your father and mother, as the LORD your God has commanded you, so that you may live long and that it may go well with you in the land the LORD your God is giving you.* (Deuteronomy 5:16)

This instruction is echoed in the New Testament:

> *"Honor your father and mother," which is the first commandment with a promise, that it may go well with you and that you may enjoy long life on the earth.* (Ephesians 6:2-3)

God has equipped parents with a special kind of love. However, throughout history, mothers have generally demonstrated this heavenly love much more noticeably. Isaiah spoke about this special motherly love:

> *Can a mother forget the baby at her breast and have no compassion on the child she has borne?* (Isaiah 49:15)

Proverbs 31 is known for its description of the ideal wife and mother. Unfortunately, this passage has been overused and abused by men in general, in an attempt to score points against their wives, mothers or girlfriends. Another verse quoted with similar intentions is:

> *Wives, submit to your husbands as to the Lord.* (Ephesians 5:22)

A passage a few verses later is often conveniently missed:

> *Husbands love your wives, just as Christ loved the church, and gave himself up for her.* (Ephesians 5:25)

What we need today is for husbands and children to constantly show their appreciation for what their wife and mother does in the home. One of the greatest weaknesses in today's families is a tendency to take each other for granted. It shouldn't take much to say "Thank you" to someone when they do something.

Now, the women reading this article should not be nodding their heads at their husbands and children, saying, "You see? You have to appreciate and respect me!" Rather, they should be trying to win the respect of their family.

> *In the same way, their wives are to be women worthy of respect, not malicious talkers but temperate and trustworthy in everything.* (1 Timothy 3:11)

What makes women special? Most men look for outward beauty and charm. However, the Bible warns:

> *Charm is deceptive, and beauty is fleeting; but a woman who fears the Lord is to be praised.* (Proverbs 31:30)

Next Mother's Day, give your mother the greatest gift: a promise to honour and appreciate her all year long. After all, she does not stop being your mother the following day!

What Is Love?

Reading: Genesis 29

For centuries, February 14 has been known as Valentine's Day. People send cards and gifts to their sweetheart, their friends or their family members. Valentine's Day comes on the feast day of two different Catholic martyrs, both named Valentine, but the customs and traditions connected with that day have nothing to do with the lives of these men.

These customs come from an ancient Roman fertility festival, Lupercalia, which took place every February 15. The festival honoured Juno, the Roman goddess of women and marriage, and Pan, the god of nature. Later, after the spread of Christianity, religious leaders tried to give Christian meaning to this pagan festival. In 496, Pope Gelasius changed the Lupercalia festival of February 15 to St. Valentine's Day on February 14. But the meaning of this pagan festival has remained unchanged to this day.

You may ask, "Is it not good to have a day of romance, affection and love?" Certainly! In fact, those things should not be limited to February 14 but, rather, celebrated every day!

The Bible is full of stories and examples of romance, affection and love.

Conjugal Love (Romance)

> *Jacob was in love with Rachel and said, "I'll work for you seven years in return for your younger daughter Rachel."… So Jacob served seven years to get Rachel, but they seemed like only a few days to him because of his love for her.* (Genesis 29:18,20)

> *Husbands, love your wives, just as Christ loved the church and gave himself up for her.* (Ephesians 5:25)

God's Love for Us

> *The Lord appeared to us in the past, saying: "I have loved you with an everlasting love; I have drawn you with loving-kindness."* (Jeremiah 31:3)

> *"For God so loved the world that he gave his one and only son, that whoever believes in him shall not perish but have eternal life."* (John 3:16)

Brotherly Love

> *This is how we know what love is: Jesus Christ laid down his life for us. And we ought to lay down our lives for our brothers.* (1 John 3:16)

Loving each other is not optional—it is a command:

> *"My command is this: Love each other as I have loved you."* (John 15:12)

If we stop loving, we will be denying God.

> *Whoever does not love does not know God, because God is love.* (1 John 4:8)

Human love, at best, is conditional, but God's love isn't!

> *But God demonstrates his own love for us in this: While we were still sinners, Christ died for us.* (Romans 5:8)

Is Valentine's Day "okay" for a Christian? Well, love is Christian and biblical. It is the very essence of our faith. So, if Valentine's Day is a day of love, then Christians should practise it every day! And live a life of love (Ephesians 5:2).

Refined Like Silver

"I will refine them like silver and test them like gold."

(1 Corinthians 7:23)

Rend Your Heart

Reading: Joel 2:12-27

Ever since I responded to an altar call in 1951, at the age of twelve, and surrendered my heart to God, inviting Christ into my life, tears of joy come to my eyes whenever I see someone come forward to confess Christ as his or her Saviour.

I have helped organize large evangelistic crusades and I have seen hundreds, even thousands, come forward to accept Jesus as their Saviour. That has been very exciting. I have also helped many individuals and couples see the need to be born-again and have prayed with them while they confessed their sins and received Christ. This always thrills my soul!

And yet, with sadness and dismay I have watched many of these new believers continue in their old sinful ways, unwilling to allow Christ to change their lives.

Depending on one's doctrinal position, there are many reasons and explanations for this, but I believe that the main reason some believers do not experience a total transformation or change is because their repentance and profession is superficial. In other words, their conversion is based on their own terms instead of on God's terms. Often, the conversion is an emotional, rather than spiritual one (see 2 Corinthians 7:10,11).

God does not expect to see an outburst of emotions and experiences. He wants to see true repentance and a broken heart.

> *"Even now,"* declares the Lord, *"return to me with all your heart, with fasting and weeping and mourning." Rend your heart and not your garments. Return to the Lord your God, for he is gracious and compassionate, slow to anger and abounding in love....* (Joel 2:12,13)

You may be a member of a church, sing in the choir, teach Sunday School or serve as a deacon. You may even be the minister of a church. Unless your heart has been broken and Christ has become your Master and Lord, you cannot be saved. Salvation is the result of true repentance, confession of sin and the forgiveness of God.

> *If my people, who are called by my name, will humble themselves and pray and seek my face and turn from their wicked ways, then will I hear from heaven and will forgive their sin and will heal their land.* (2 Chronicles 7:14)

Lack of holiness is our problem. We, as individuals and as churches, cannot and will not prosper spiritually until we pray and ask for a revival. We need to be revived if we want to find total peace, joy and meaning for our lives and if we want to bring others to the saving knowledge of Jesus Christ.

Are you ready for a revival? More importantly, do you want a revival?

Sinners Saved by Grace!

Reading: Romans 3:21-31

Some time ago I was watching a European television program called "The Jungle". Its main purpose is to expose, debate and attack corruption. This particular episode was about religion and there were representatives from the three main Christian groups, as well as communists and politicians. For about two hours, the religious leaders of the Greek Orthodox, Catholic and Protestant churches argued, often accusing each other in a mean-spirited way.

At one point, the program host turned to a man who claimed to be a communist and atheist and asked him to comment. The man smiled and sarcastically responded, "Well, what can I say? Look at them. They claim to be Christians, but they are at each other's throats, trying to gouge out each other's eyes."

While these men each tried to prove that he was right and the others were wrong, viewers probably wondered whether Jesus Christ is able to change the human heart.

This is not an uncommon situation. While our church leaders are busy measuring sins to see who is committing bigger and more terrible sins, classifying those people as bad sinners, lost people are heading toward eternal death without Christ.

Of course, the terms "bad sin" or "bad sinner" doesn't even make any sense. Are there "good sins" or "good sinners"? No, of course not! Sin is sin and any transgression is bad enough to separate us from a holy and righteous God for all eternity (Romans 3:23).

All our righteous acts are like filthy rags. (Isaiah 64:6)

We all need the saving grace of God. It makes no difference how few sins we may have committed, or how we may be in the eyes of others. God knows our hearts and our lives.

"Adultery and murder are terrible sins," someone may say. Yes, but so are gossiping and judging. Until we are willing to admit our guilt, we are just as guilty as anyone else, no matter how good we may appear to be.

Dear reader, if you are not sure about your standing in the Body of Christ and if you have doubts about your salvation, place your trust in Christ the Saviour who died on the cross for your sins. You can know complete forgiveness and deliverance through faith in Jesus Christ.

No, there are no "good sinners". Sin is sin and it separates us from God. Your small sins and the "big bad" sins of your brothers are sins just the same. Actually, we are all bad sinners... but through faith in Christ, we can be justified.

Just remember that the world around us is watching to see whether the gospel of Jesus Christ has made a difference in our lives. Has Christ made a difference in your daily life? Have you confessed your sins to God—all of them, small and big—and asked Him to forgive you?

True Religion

Reading: 1 John 3:11-24

More and more, people are becoming confused by the plethora of religions in the world today. New religions and cults seem to be popping up all over the place. Little wonder that many have given up religion altogether.

Suppose, however, that I have never been exposed to any religion, although I know that there are many. One day I decide to choose a religion for myself. How do I go about this task? How do I distinguish the true religion from the others?

Pretending to be in this situation, I went to the library and found a book entitled "Great Religions of the World", published by the National Geographic Society. The table of contents listed five religions and described their main themes as follows:

HINDUISM: Quest for the universal one, 33 million gods....

BUDDHISM: The eight-fold path to Nirvana (state of bliss or emptiness, the zero and infinity)....

JUDAISM: "Hear O Israel" (law)....

ISLAM: Mohammed is the prophet....

CHRISTIANITY: "I am the Resurrection and the Life"....

Of course, these are not the only religions that exist—there are thousands of others. These are, according to the National Geographic Society, the "great" religions. Fine, but I am not looking for a great religion. I am looking for the true religion.

I decided to read about all of these listed religions, but one of them already had my attention... the last one. The last one makes my heart beat faster. It offers resurrection and life! This one's leader claimed to be God and, unlike the others, the "prophet" is God's Son... and He's alive!

Reading further, I found out that Christianity is very complicated, divided into many small groups, one different from the other. At this point, can you imagine how confused someone might become? They might go from church to church, trying to find the truth and life only to find more confusion.

What is the secret of life and happiness, of peace and fulfillment? Observe this conversation:

> *"Teacher, which is the greatest commandment in the Law?" Jesus replied, "'Love the Lord your God with all your heart and with all your soul and with all your mind.' This is the first and greatest commandment. And the second is like it: 'Love your neighbour as yourself.' All the law and the prophets hang on these two commandments."* (Matthew 22:36-40)

What an eye-opener! True religion isn't religion at all. It is a way of life that revolves around and is filled with the Spirit of the one Living God. Religion alone can save no one!

To learn what God says about religion, read Micah 6:8, Hosea 6:6, Matthew 7:21, Mark 7:6, James 1:27, John 13:34-35 and 1 John 3:23-24. May He help you to find the truth and life, too!

God Hates Religion, Too!

Reading: Matthew 23

Very often I will initiate a conversation with a customer in my store, which usually leads to sharing my testimony or a few words about life and death.

Some people respond in a cordial and positive way while others avoid the subject. Many reply: "Oh well, I don't want to talk about religion," or "I hate religion and churches" or "I don't like religions and I don't want to support them."

I respond by saying, "I, too, don't like religions and you know what? God does not like religions either. As a matter of fact, God never started a religion or established a religious organization." This usually surprises them and earns me a smile of satisfaction because they think that they are off the hook. However, before they say another word, I usually add: "But, you know, just because man-made religions have messed up people's lives and done more harm than good, it does not mean that there is no God and a way to find Him."

Now, I have their attention. They hate religions and their establishments, but they are ready to at least talk about God and Jesus. The reasons or excuses for being so negative and hostile about the Church or religions are very predictable and invariably the same:

"Religion is big business." "Religion gave me nothing more than rules and regulations." "They kept us blind, empty and thirsty." "They talk about salvation, but we find nothing that gives something to hold on to." "Religion has cheated us."

These are only some of the comments people make when I start talking to them about God. It is so sad to hear people reject

Jesus Christ and His gospel and blame religion and church. The Bible says:

> *Everyone who calls on the name of the Lord will be saved.* (Romans 10:13)

The question is:

> *How, then, can they call on the one they have not believed in? And how can they believe in the One of whom they have not heard? And how can they hear without someone preaching to them?* (Romans 10:14)

How can we, who know the truth, not be partly or even totally guilty for not preaching, teaching and sharing the truth to them? How can we be so relaxed, enjoying the trip while eternal souls are heading toward eternal death in hell? What will the churches and shepherds say to God for destroying and scattering the sheep?

Listen to the words of God:

> *"Woe to the shepherds who are destroying and scattering the sheep of my pasture!" declares the LORD. Therefore this is what the LORD, the God of Israel, says to the shepherds who tend my people: "Because you have scattered my flock and driven them away and have not bestowed care on them, I will bestow punishment on you for the evil you have done," declares the LORD.* (Jeremiah 23:1-2)

Someone may say, "Oh well, that was in the Old Testament." Well, then listen to what Jesus said in the New Testament:

> *"Woe to you, teachers of the law and Pharisees, you hypocrites! You shut the kingdom of heaven in men's face. You yourselves do not enter, nor will you let those enter who are trying to. Woe to you, teachers of the law*

and Pharisees, you hypocrites! You travel over land and sea to win a single convert, and when he becomes one, you make him twice as much a son of hell as you are." (Matthew 23:13-15)

In fact, all of chapter 23 should be a warning to us.

If Jesus gave His life for the Church, for us, then what kind of church should the Church be? What kind of message should it preach?

If we look at the believers in Acts, we will see why they were so blessed and effective in spreading the Good News of the gospel of Jesus Christ. It says:

> *After they prayed, the place where they were meeting was shaken. And they were all filled with the Holy Spirit and spoke the word of God boldly. All the believers were one in heart and mind. No one claimed that any of his possessions was his own, but they shared everything they had. With great power the apostles continued to testify to the resurrection of the Lord Jesus, and much grace was upon them all.* (Acts 4:31-33)

Christ expects nothing less than holiness from the Church and the believers. He expects the Church to preach nothing more or nothing less than the true gospel.

The Angel of God gave strict instructions to the apostles:

> *"Go, stand in the temple courts," he said, "and tell the people the full message of this new life." At the daybreak they entered the temple courts, as they had been told, and began to teach the people. When the high priest and his associates arrived, they called together the Sanhedrin—the full assembly of the elders of Israel—and sent to the jail for the apostles.* (Acts 5:20-21)

Should the Church today preach less than *"the full message of this new life"*? I believe that every church leader and every believer must answer this question.

Coffee Break

Religion vs. Christ

Religion enslaves.
Christ liberates!

Religion condemns.
Christ pardons!

Religion brings tears.
Christ wipes tears away!

Religion leaves a heart empty.
Christ fills the empty heart!

Religion searches for meaning in life.
Christ gives meaning to life!

Religion asks questions.
Christ is the answer!

Religion seeks truth.
Christ is the truth.

Religion Does Not Save— Christ Does

Reading: John 5:31-47

I have met people who proudly declare that they have read the Bible many times, have studied religions and even have a few degrees in religious studies… but when it comes to their own personal relationship with God, they either avoid the subject or are not sure.

A gentleman started coming to our Bible study some time ago. He was a very educated person who had been studying the Bible for many years. He had also studied eastern religions and theology. He knew the Bible so well that he would quote Bible verses for us. He believed that, by studying and learning about God and spiritual things, a person could obtain eternal life.

What would upset him more than anything else was the fact that we would refer to Jesus as our Lord and Saviour. He would talk about Jesus and pray to Jesus, but he would only refer to Him as a great man. He did not believe that Jesus could save.

There are many today who claim to believe in Jesus. They study the Scriptures, they even teach and preach the Scriptures, but, sadly, they will not ask Jesus to save them.

Jesus said:

> *"You diligently study the Scriptures because you think that by them you possess eternal life. These are the scriptures that testify about me, yet you refuse to come to me to have life…. I have come in my Father's name, and you do not accept me; but if someone else comes in his own name, you will accept him."* (John 5:39-40,43)

It is terrible to think that so many men and women who have the Scriptures in their hands and diligently study them could be so blind. But it is even more inexcusable that, after the Lord Jesus speaks to them through godly people or the Holy Spirit, they still refuse to accept Him.

The real reason people do not accept Jesus is not because they cannot understand the Bible or because they find it impossible to believe in Jesus. There is nothing about Jesus Christ that makes it impossible for them to trust Him. The real reason and fault is in man's own will. He loves his way of life more than he loves Jesus the Saviour. He wants to have eternal life but also to keep the world and the worldly ways of life.

Have you discovered Jesus in the Scriptures? And if you have, has He become your Lord and Saviour?

What Can Satisfy Our Thirst?
Reading: Psalm 42

The world is full of religion. In fact, there is so much religion that people don't know what to do with it. Have religions changed the world for the better? Have religions made the spiritual hunger of people go away or have they made it worse?

In spite of the increase and sophistication of religions with state-of-the-art equipment and technology, the human heart is hungrier than ever for the truth! The effects of spiritual hunger are more painful and longer lasting than those of physical hunger. The human soul hungers and thirsts for spiritual food, for God.

King David had everything a man could ever desire—power, prestige, wealth and family—but listen to his words:

> *As the deer pants for streams of water, so my soul pants for you, O God. My soul thirsts for God, for the living God. When can I go and meet with God?* (Psalm 42:1-2)

We don't have to go very far today to find people that are hungry and thirsty for spiritual things. But why has religion not been able to satisfy that hunger? Isn't that what religion is supposed to do? Man-made religion has never been able to satisfy that uniquely human need and feel the vacuum of the human heart. Only God can do that.

In the Old Testament, God invited all those who were spiritually hungry and thirsty to come to Him.

> *Come, all you who are thirsty, come to the waters; and you who have no money, come, buy and eat! Come, buy… without money and without cost.* (Isaiah 55:1)

Jesus repeats that invitation many times in the New Testament.

> *"If a man is thirsty, let him come to me and drink."* (John 7:37)

> *"I am the bread of life. He who comes to me will never go hungry, and he who believes in me will never be thirsty."* (John 6:35)

As a matter of fact, Jesus goes as far as to say that the water He gives will become an eternal spring of life in the person who drinks it. Let's look at that verse:

> *"But whoever drinks the water I give him will never thirst. Indeed, the water I give him will become in him a spring of water welling up to eternal life."* (John 4:14)

No, man-made religions will not, cannot, quench the human

thirst and satisfy the heart. And no, religions and their religious activities cannot guarantee total and continuous satisfaction of the heart. Only God can!

> *"Never again will they hunger; never again will they thirst."* (Revelation 7:16)

The last words of the Bible are an invitation given to the human race:

> *The Spirit and the bride say, "Come!" And let him who hears say, "Come!" Whoever is thirsty, let him come; and whoever wishes, let him take the free gift of the water of life.* (Revelation 22:17)

The Experiment Failed

Reading: Matthew 9:14-17

What experiment? The experiment of the "Easy Gospel," of the "Wide Way" instead of the "Narrow Way," of salvation without repentance and condemnation of the old person and life. In other words, cheap and easy "believism".

Why was this experiment tried? Because churches wanted to fill their pews with people, to help their children remain in the Church and to help other young people come in without upsetting them. It was an effort to keep people in our churches and not lose them to other activities. We wanted to have our churches full—not because we wanted to fill heaven with redeemed people, but to show off, to satisfy our pride and selfishness and to feel good and blessed by being surrounded with so many people who were feeling good and happy.

In other words, the aim was not to glorify God and His holy name, but it was our own gratification, glory and comfort. We compromised and weakened the gospel, God's truth and the law of His holiness. We thought we could do it our way, using our own intelligence and techniques, our own materials and inventions. We did it our way, not the way of the Bible. We tried and we tried hard. We relied on our inner feelings, emotions and experiences—without paying attention to God and His truth—because it suited our plans and way of life. In the business world, this is called counterfeiting.

How do we know that the experiment failed? The answer is clear, but where do we start—in the home, in the church, in the workplace?

The divorce rate has skyrocketed among Christians. Many children from so-called Christian families have very little, if any, spirituality or the desire for holiness. They love themselves and the world. This is also true among the young adults and older men and women in our churches.

They do not worship God only. They worship their own gods, too. They go away from Christ without a second thought; they leave Him and they take Him back as if Christ and His death on the cross can be taken or left at our own whim. In essence, they are people who are not born-again. They are not saved. Christ is not reflected in their lives.

There are those who wanted to know Christ and the power of His resurrection without wanting to consider everything as rubbish and loss (Philippians 3:7-10) and without giving up any of the worldly things for the sake of Christ. They wanted to follow Him without first denying themselves. They wanted to receive eternal life without giving up worldly things and habits, like *"sewing a patch of unshrunk cloth on an old garment"* or *"pouring new wine into old wineskins"* (Matthew 9:15-17).

Now that the experiment has failed, the tears have started to flow. Children are lost, churches are dead and people with compromised lives are in and out of churches, not knowing what they want.

Failure of easy "believism". The results stun and shock us. The tears are almost too late to change and turn things around. These tears should have been shed at the right time. But there is still a ray of hope. If we turn back to the Bible and if we humble ourselves and pray and seek His face and turn from our wicked ways, then He will hear from heaven and will forgive our sins and will heal our land (2 Chronicles 7:14).

We must also start letting Him do the talking while we listen. If we really love Him, His glory, His will and His Kingdom, then the direction of things can change. Humility, repentance and a surrendered life are the only things that will bring holiness into our lives, homes and churches.

But for this to happen, we must become lovers of the truth—and the truth will set us free. If we don't love the truth, we will not be blessed and our tears and prayers will not be answered.

Watch Out for Counterfeits!

Reading: 1 Thessalonians 5:12-28

Counterfeiting is one of the most profitable and widely spread forms of crime. Every coin or bill is either genuine or counterfeit. Even if it is almost like the original, it is still counterfeit. And the more it looks and feels like the real thing, the more dangerous the counterfeit is.

Money is not the only thing that is counterfeited. Paintings, jewels, watches, T-shirts, clothing, etc. are also counterfeited. As a matter of fact, all good or valuable things seem to be counterfeited—not only in the natural world, but also in the spiritual world.

> *Test everything. Hold on to the good.* (1 Thessalonians 5:21)

Jesus also warned His followers against counterfeits:

> *"Watch out! Be on your guard."* (Luke 12:1)

COUNTERFEIT GODS

Idolatry was a common sin of Israel. The first commandment says,

> *"You shall have no other gods before me. You shall not make for yourself an idol."* (Exodus 20:3-4)

An idol is not only an image made of metal or stone. It can be (and usually is) a mental image—the love of money, material things, fame, prestige, pleasure, even a religion.

COUNTERFEIT CHRISTS

Jesus warned:

> *"For false Christs and false prophets will appear and perform great signs and miracles to deceive even the elect—if that were possible. See, I have told you ahead of time."* (Matthew 24:24-25)

There have been, and still are, many that claim to be Jesus Christ.

COUNTERFEIT PROPHETS AND TEACHERS

> *"Watch out for false prophets. They come to you in sheep's clothing, but inwardly they are ferocious wolves."* (Matthew 7:15)

Counterfeit Gospel

> *I am astonished that you are so quickly deserting the one who called you by the grace of Christ and are turning to a different gospel—which is really no gospel at all. Evidently some people are throwing you into confusion and are trying to pervert the gospel of Christ.* (Galatians 1:6-7)

Counterfeit Faith

Many will say that as long as you have faith, you're okay. That's like saying that as long you have medication you'll get better. But if you use the wrong medication, not only will you not get better, but you could also be putting yourself in danger! True faith is believing and trusting in the One and Only Living God and His Son Jesus Christ and His gospel.

Counterfeit Christians

Those who follow and accept counterfeit teachers and their false gospels eventually become counterfeit Christians.

The only way to know what is genuine and true is by studying the original carefully. Study the Word of God daily.

Busy—but We Can't Fool God

Reading: Matthew 6:1-6; 23:13-18

Looking busy and being involved in many religious activities may impress people around us, but we can't fool God about our faith, our character or our service. Christ was not fooled by the role-playing and the activities of the Pharisees, whom He denounced in Matthew 23:13-18.

He called them hypocrites. In other words, they were actors, playing several parts, just as a theatre's actors play several parts. To change identities, they would simply wear a different mask. They were putting on a performance to win the applause of the community. They didn't care what they were deep inside.

Jesus warned us not to be like the hypocrites, who perform their religious "duties" to be seen by others (Matthew 6:1-6).

We may appear to be busy practising "churchianity". We may even appear to be sincerely religious. But God knows if our profession is just acting or genuine devotion. We cannot impress God with the masks we wear and the roles we play.

Jesus condemned hypocrisy more than any other sin—especially the shameless, self-righteous kind practised by the religious leaders of His day. Religious hypocrites are unholy fakes who try to fool people—but they cannot fool God.

Are you a church-going, religious person who is depending on your own good works to gain eternal life? Or are you a born-again follower of Jesus Christ our Lord? Do you have the assurance of your salvation and are you relying on Christ the Saviour?

Just remember we can't fool God. Playing the role well is not enough!

Will a Man Rob God?

Reading: 2 Corinthians 8:1-15

A common complaint among both believers and unbelievers is: "There are too many out there asking for more of my money." Using this as an excuse, some cut down their offerings while others stop giving altogether. It is this general attitude that hurts honest churches and people who are in real need.

In chapters eight and nine of 2 Corinthians, we see a good example of how churches must respond to the needs of the poor. Paul boldly tells believers about their financial responsibility toward the needy and toward the church. He himself had given up everything.

Talking about giving or tithing today is risky. People are very sensitive about giving because of the abuses they've seen. However, a church cannot fulfill two of its greatest responsibilities—helping the poor and evangelizing—without the financial support of believers.

Those who rob God are depriving themselves of "the privilege of sharing".

> *"Will a man rob God? Yet you rob me. But you ask, 'How do we rob you?' In tithes and offerings. You are under a curse—the whole nation of you—because you are robbing me. Bring the whole tithe into the storehouse, that there may be food in my house. Test me in this,"* says the Lord Almighty, *"and see if I will not throw open the floodgates of heaven and pour out so much blessing that you will not have room enough for it."* (Malachi 3:8-10)

It isn't only the rich who can give. Luke 21:1-4 tells the story of the poor widow who placed two small copper coins into the temple treasury. We see in this story that Jesus was more impressed with her gift than with the large amounts that the rich gave. Her offering was from her heart.

There can be joy in giving. When we give ourselves to the Lord, we want to do His will. Because of this, giving to others comes very naturally.

In 2 Corinthians 8:7, Paul exhorted and encouraged the believers in Corinth to increase in the gift of giving. He then explained why:

> *For you know the grace of our Lord Jesus Christ, that though he was rich, yet for your sakes he became poor, so that you through his poverty might become rich. (2 Corinthians 8:9)*

Finally,

> *Remember this: Whoever sows sparingly will also reap sparingly, and whoever sows generously will also reap generously. Each man should give what he has decided in his heart to give, not reluctantly or under compulsion, for God loves a cheerful giver. (2 Corinthians 9:6-7)*

Jesus Saw
Reading: Mark 12:41-44

"Giving" is a very touchy subject nowadays, especially in connection with the Church. However, it must have been important to Jesus because, in Mark 12, we see Him sitting opposite the treasury, watching as people gave money. What did He see?

He saw the rich giving. Jesus did not judge the gifts of the rich. In fact, He had several wealthy friends and followers. Being rich is not wrong—but being obsessed by wealth is. God expects us to give according to our means.

He saw the poor giving. Jesus watched as a poor widow placed two small coins into the treasury. These coins were worth less than a penny, yet Jesus was immediately impressed.

Why? Why wasn't He impressed by the large amounts the rich people gave? It is possible that some people scoffed when they saw how little the widow gave. But Jesus knew how much she could afford and He knew the spirit with which she gave.

Imagine the scene: rich people march in, dig into their pouches to scoop up a handful of coins and throw them into the treasury. Hear the noise of all those copper coins! How many heads turn to see who is giving so generously? Then a widow comes in, probably unnoticed, and carefully puts in her two coins.

Suddenly Jesus decides it's lesson time for His disciples. He points out the differences in those who gave. The rich threw in their offering—proudly and disrespectfully. The widow came close and humbly gave her gift. The rich gave from their leftovers. The widow gave all she had.

Next time you put aside a portion for Him, remember that the Lord sees—not only what we give, but also how we give it. Remember: you are not giving to people but to God.

> *Honor the Lord with your wealth, with the firstfruits of all your crops.* (Proverbs 3:9)

Jesus Has Everything to Do with It!

Reading: Luke 4:14-30

Recently I was listening to a round-table debate about religion and politics. Politicians, church leaders and theologians were all vigorously debating the place of religion in politics and culture. While everyone was trying to make his or her point about the importance of the Christian religion and preserving the Christian tradition and culture, someone asked a question about Jesus. One of the leaders responded: "What does Jesus have to do with this now? Leave Jesus out of this!"

It seems that many religious people and leaders are more interested in and more devoted to the Christian religion than to Christ. They will spend more time and energy defending and preserving religious and cultural traditions than spreading the Good News that God loved the world and sent His only Son Jesus to save everyone who believes in Him.

The world rejected Jesus then and many continue to reject Him today.

> *Then the whole town went out to meet Jesus, and when they saw Him, they pleaded with Him to leave their region.* (Matthew 8:34)

Jesus was bad for business. But look at what happened to Him in the synagogue when He stood up and said,

> *"The spirit of the Lord is on me because He has anointed me to preach the good news to the poor. He has sent me to proclaim freedom for the prisoners and recovery of sight for the blind, to release the oppressed."* (Luke 4:18)
>
> *All the people in the synagogue were furious when they heard this. They got up, drove him out of the town, and took him to the brow of the hill… to throw him down the cliff. But Jesus walked right through the crowd and went on his way.* (Luke 4:28-30)

Please remember that these were religious people and leaders. They were all practising and going through the motions of religion. But when Jesus spoke, they wanted to get rid of Him. It was okay for Jesus to be there as long as He kept quiet, as long as He did not bother them with His messages, and as long as He did not rock the boat.

Many feel the same way today. Church is fine, activities are great and fellowship is wonderful… as long as you leave Jesus out of them, as long as you don't rock the boat with messages that upset and bother us.

When Jesus was rejected, He *"walked right through the crowd and went on His way."* Jesus will not stay where He is not wanted… especially when churches and their members don't want to hear His voice.

Are we letting Jesus speak or are we doing all the talking? Are you ready to say, like Samuel, *"Speak, Lord, for your servant is listening"*?

Is Christ Divided?

Reading: 1 Corinthians 1

You are eager to share your faith with others. You go out of your way to meet someone that will be willing to listen to your testimony and perhaps ask you to show him how to become a born-again Christian like you.

You greet the person sitting next to you in the doctor's office and somehow you bring up the subject of your faith. He tells you that he is a Christian and a member of a well-known church. He then says, "So, you are a Christian. That's good. What are you? I mean are you Protestant?" And before you can even answer, he comes up with other questions like: "What church do you go to? What is your doctrine like? Are you Calvinist or Arminian? What Bible translation do you read? What organization is your church affiliated with?"

You are sorry you started the conversation. You feel intimidated and you want to say: "All I know is that I was blind and now I see, I was lost and now I am found. Let me introduce to you Jesus Christ, my Lord and Saviour."

That's exactly how Paul felt. Writing to the Corinthians, he said:

> *One of you says, "I follow Paul"; another, "I follow Apollos"; another "I follow Cephas"; still another, "I follow Christ." Is Christ divided? Was Paul crucified for you? Were you baptized into the name of Paul?* (1 Corinthians 1:12-13)

When people ask me about my religion, I tell them I don't have one and I don't need one. I have Christ—the only way, the only door and the only life. I tell them that I am washed in the blood of Jesus Christ, forgiven, redeemed and saved from eternal damnation and that I will soon go to meet my Creator and Lord.

Apostle Paul's desire was to meet his Creator. He said,

> *I have fought the good fight, I have finished the race, I have kept the faith. Now there is in store for me the crown of righteousness… not only to me, but also to all who have longed for His appearing.* (2 Timothy 4:7-8)

Is this your desire too?

The Unknown God

Reading: Acts 17:16-34

Athens has always been famous for being a religious and cultural centre. However, the Apostle Paul only saw sin and superstition. In fact, as one ancient writer put it, "It was easier to find an idol than a man in Athens."

In those days, Athens was controlled by two main

philosophies: Stoicism and Epicureanism. The Stoics were materialistic and fatalistic. Nature was their god and they believed that the only use for knowledge was to help a person find his place in nature. The Epicureans were followers of Epicurus, a Greek philosopher who taught that pleasure is good and pain is evil. These people were atheistic.

Paul was in the midst of two extremely different philosophies. This led him to the Areopagus, the official court (also called Mar's Hill). There Paul preached a great sermon about good news.

He began politely, saying, *"I see that you are very religious...."* He went on to point out the altar "To the Unknown God". He then presented to them the true and living God who was still unknown to them. He presented four great truths about God:

GOD IS THE CREATOR

The Greeks believed different theories about creation, including some forms of evolution. Paul clearly tells them that God has created everything and that He doesn't live in men's temples. He gives life to all and man really cannot give Him anything.

GOD IS THE GOVERNOR

God controls the nations and people everywhere. Again, Paul very diplomatically pointed out that their temples and images were useless and foolish.

GOD IS THE SAVIOUR

Paul wiped away the great Greek culture by calling it *"times of ignorance!"* With all their wisdom and culture, the people failed to find God.

GOD IS THE JUDGE

God has appointed a Day of Judgment and His judge will be His Son, Jesus Christ.

> *This will take place on the day when God will judge men's secrets through Jesus Christ, as the gospel declares.* (Romans 2:16)

The Greeks' reactions were mixed: some made fun of Paul and others delayed, but a few believed! One of the converts was an important member of the court named Dionysius.

This portion in Acts presents three different attitudes toward the gospel and we find these same attitudes in society today. Some openly oppose the Word of God. Some mock it or postpone making a decision about it. A small number receive and believe. What about you?

The Church Must Be an Oasis
Reading: Revelation 3:1-6

If Jesus was visiting your town or city and wanted to go to church, what kind of church would He look for? If He called ahead of time for information, what do you suppose His questions would be?

Do you think He would want to know what denomination your church belongs to? The size of the congregation? Which Bible version you use? How large you choir is? How long the service lasts? The skin colour of the members? The size of the kitchen or gym? Whether there is a bazaar once in awhile?

I have been asked these very questions by people who were interested in visiting or attending our church. To be fair, there have been a few who have asked me about our beliefs and spiritual condition.

When Jesus visited Jerusalem, He went to the temple to

worship, but they were having a bazaar. They had turned it into a shopping centre.

Jesus did not want to hear any of their excuses or reasons for doing this. Instead,

> *He began driving out all those who were buying and selling there. He overturned the tables... and the benches... and would not allow anyone to carry merchandise through the temple courts.* (Mark 11:15-16)

And He said:

> *"'My house will be called a house of prayer'... But you have made it a 'den of robbers.'"* (Mark 11:17)

I wonder: if Jesus were to visit our churches today, what would He say or do? I can only wonder and guess. I believe that the Church does not exist for itself and its own entertainment, but it should be a mission outpost to help people find God and make peace with Him.

The Church must be an oasis in the middle of a spiritual desert to quench the spiritually thirsty. The Church should be a burning bush to remind people that they are standing on holy ground, whenever they gather around His throne to worship Him. The Church must be a spiritual clinic to help the spiritually weak and suffering.

The Church must be all this and more. What the Church must not be is a private social club, a place of entertainment or a business.

Listen to what Jesus said to the church of Sardis:

> *"I know your deeds; you have a reputation of being alive, but you are dead. Wake up! Strengthen what remains and is about to die, for I have not found your deeds complete in the sight of my God."* (Revelation 3:1-2)

He concluded with the words:

> *"He who has an ear, let him hear what the Spirit says to the churches."* (Revelation 3:6)

Are we and our churches ready to receive a visit from Jesus Christ our Lord?

The Going, Growing Church
Reading: Acts 4:31-33

"What's the matter with the churches? Why are they closing down?" someone asked me recently. It would seem as though God has turned away and rejected the Church. Well, it may be true that God has walked away from some churches because of their sin, worldliness, corruption and lack of Christ-likeness.

Let's look at the early church—a going and growing church. It was a church aflame—from 120 to 10 million members in one century. It had few of the tools we consider necessary today: no printing presses or media ministries, no sound systems, no professional clergymen and leaders, not even church buildings.

But those early believers outdid us and would put us to shame today. With all our technological progress and education and organizational skills put together, we still don't do well. Why not? What did that church have that we need?

It Was a Praying Church

The church was born in a prayer meeting. Both men and women prayed in one accord (Acts 1:14). They prayed and they were filled with the Holy Spirit (Acts 4:31).

When Peter was in jail they prayed (Acts 12). They prayed with such faith that it made them bold. They prayed so fervently that the building was shaken.

Prayer is vital if the Church is to move ahead. The church that is not praying is playing. The church is powerless without prayer.

It Was a Loving Church

Love made them share with others. Love enabled them to give to those in need. Love enabled them to put away their differences. Today, minor differences divided and cripple the Church. Love united them. This kind of love brings revival. They loved things of above more than earthly possessions.

It Was a Witnessing Church

Jesus had promised that power would be given to all the believers who received the Holy Spirit to become His witnesses (Acts 1:8). And, of course, there was the Great Commission (Matthew 28:19). David Dawson said, "The silent pew is the curse and blight of Christianity."

When the Apostles were arrested and thrown into jail, "an angel of the Lord came during the night and opened the doors and brought them out"—not to go home and hide, not to warn other members of the church to be quiet and politically correct—but to

> ... *go stand in the temple courts and tell the people the full message of this new life.* (Acts 5:20)

And that's exactly what they did—immediately.

I believe that many have forgotten or misunderstood the purpose and role of the Church. One Protestant denomination in Canada has decided to be politically correct and, at their general council meeting, proposed to "reject and repudiate all mission and proselytism seeking to convert Jews to Christianity."

Dear friends, let's not forget that the New Testament Church was not established by Gentiles, but by Jesus Christ and His disciples, who were Jews. They brought the gospel to the rest of the world and now, many so-called "Christian" churches are ignoring and rejecting the Great Commission to go and evangelize all the nations.

Why does today's Church have so little impact? I believe the reasons are many, but let me give you some that are obvious:

- Too many spectators, not enough workers and doers.
- Too much interest in the methods and not enough in the message.
- Too much concern about public image and not enough about the truth and godliness.
- Little or no concern for the lost and winning them to Christ.
- Few evangelistic meetings. Evangelism is largely forgotten today.
- Settling for lesser causes.
- Disregard and neglect of our mission.

Jesus' words, *"You will be my witnesses in Jerusalem and in all Judea and Samaria and to the ends of the earth,"* seem to have been forgotten. But the world needs to hear the gospel today more than ever before. Let's respond to that need.

We must not ever forget that we have the gospel because of those who were unstoppable. They—praying, loving and witnessing—marched ahead. We have the same marching orders. They changed the world. So can we.

Why Does the Church Exist?

Reading: Matthew 28

Most of us have thought about the Church at one time or another and we have our own opinions about it. We need to find out, though, what God's will is for the Church.

The Church belongs to Christ. He founded her, died for her, sent the Holy Spirit to her and will one day return for her. As owner of the Church, Jesus has already established her purpose and principles—and these are not negotiable. Our duty is to understand the purpose Christ has for the Church and then to put it into practice.

Jesus summarized the purpose of the Church with a commandment:

> *"'Love the Lord your God with all your heart and with all your soul and with all your mind'.... And... 'Love your neighbour as yourself.'"* (Matthew 22:37-40)

... and with a commission:

> *"Go and make disciples of all nations, baptizing them in the name of the Father and of the Son and of the Holy Spirit, and teaching them to obey everything I have commanded you."* (Matthew 28:19-20)

These two verses must define everything we do in our churches. If an activity or program fulfills one of these instructions, we must do it. If it doesn't, we must not do it. In His instructions, Jesus gave His Church five tasks to accomplish:

Love the Lord with All Your Heart

The instruction here is to *worship*. The Church exists to worship God.

> *"Worship the Lord your God, and serve Him."* (Matthew 4:10)

Notice that worship comes before service. Sometimes we are so busy with the work of the Lord that we neglect the Lord of the work.

Love Your Neighbour as Yourself

The instruction here is for *ministry*. The Church exists to demonstrate God's love to others by reaching out to them, meeting their needs and healing their hearts in the name of Jesus.

Go and Make Disciples

This is called *evangelism*. The Church exists to communicate God's Word, to be ambassadors for Christ. It is every Christian's responsibility to share the Good News wherever he or she goes.

Baptize Them

Why is baptism so important that it is included in the Great Commission? It symbolizes *fellowship* and identification with the Body of Christ. As Christians, we are called to belong, not just believe.

Teach Them to Obey

This is *discipleship*. The Church exists to edify and educate God's people, helping them to become more like Christ in every way.

A good example of these five principles being applied is the first church in Jerusalem (Acts 2). They taught each other, had fellowship together, worshipped, ministered and evangelized. Today, the purpose of the Church remains the same.

"What's in It for Me?"
Reading: Matthew 19:16-30

A while ago I met a couple who had just immigrated to Canada from East Europe. When I asked them about their religious background, they said that they had recently become Christians and had hoped to find a good church when they moved to Canada so they could learn more about God and Jesus Christ.

However, when they came to Canada, they were a little disappointed because their vision or concept of a Christian Church was not what they found here in North America. They thought a Christian church was a place where you go to worship God, feel His presence, hear His voice and meet others who are eager to do the same.

They were surprised to find that the few churches they went to seemed to be more interested in church business, entertainment and comfort, rather than making the churchgoer feel that he or she was in God's presence and that He should be honoured. In other words, they felt that people were more interested in what they would get out of their visit to church than in what they could offer to God!

To the world, the prayers and worship activities of many Christians may be seen as religious activities for personal gain or approval. Many believers expect and even demand God to bless them, heal them and reward them because they go to church regularly, they pray, they give to the church and so on. I hope you would agree with me that we, who have been redeemed by the blood of Jesus Christ and are members of the Body of Christ, must not worship God for our own benefit.

Dear reader, our worship of God, our Lord and Saviour, should not be done so that we can gain something. Instead, every thought or action should be done out of honour for Him and His greatness and because He has already blessed us and saved us and is preparing a place for us. How can we ever say that we do not benefit when we turn our lives over to Him? Of course, we do! But that should not be our motivation.

We should not worship God to gain His benefits—we already have them!

The Church

Reading: Colossians 1:15-23

The Church is the "Universal Body" made up of all the believers in Jesus Christ—from the Pentecost up to the Rapture. But there is also the local body, the local church. Most of the 112 references in the New Testament to the "Church" refer to a local congregation of baptized believers.

> *For we were all baptized by one Spirit into one body—whether Jews or Greeks, slave or free—and we were all given the one Spirit to drink.* (1 Corinthians 12:13)

The head of the Church is Christ.

> *And he is the head of the body, the church; he is the beginning and the firstborn from among the dead, so that in everything he might have the supremacy.* (Colossians 1:18)

A body without a head is dead. A church that does not have Christ as its head is dead! The head of the one "Universal Body" (the Church) is Jesus Christ and that same head, Christ, is the head of each local church.

It is important for the church to have a balanced ministry of the Word of God and prayer. The Word of God instructs the church; prayer inspires the church to obey the Word of God. The church that has a lot of Bible teaching but little prayer will have much light but no heat. It will be a doctrinally correct church, but it will be frozen! On the other hand, the church that has much prayer and religious enthusiasm but little teaching from the Word of God produces a group of people with zeal but no knowledge.

In 1 Timothy 2, Apostle Paul lists prayer as *"first of all"*— not second or third. The local church does not pray because it is the expected thing to do, but because prayer is vital to its life. The Holy Spirit works in the local church through prayer and the Word of God.

> *They devoted themselves to the apostles' teaching and to the fellowship, to the breaking of bread and to prayer.* (Acts 2:42)

> *After they prayed, the place where they were meeting was shaken. And they were all filled with the Holy Spirit and spoke the word of God boldly.* (Acts 4:31)

The church that prays will have power and will make a lasting impact for Christ. When I talk about a praying church, I am not referring only to the church "organization" or the pastor, but all the church members, all the true believers.

> *I want men everywhere to lift up holy hands in prayer, without anger or disputing.* (1 Timothy 2:8)

Church members should live godly, holy lives. God expects certain things from believers who, although in this world and affected by the things of this world, are not to conform to the evil things of this world.

> *Therefore, I urge you, brothers, in view of God's mercy, to offer your bodies as living sacrifices, holy and pleasing to God—this is your spiritual act of worship. Do not conform any longer to the pattern of this world, but be transformed by the renewing of your mind. Then you will be able to test and approve what God's will is— his good, pleasing and perfect will.* (Romans 12:1-2)

The church congregation that does not aim to accomplish holiness and purity is heading toward disaster. The unity and fellowship of believers is also key to the strength of the local church. A church without a real spirit of fellowship is like a paralyzed body—alive but unable to function effectively.

Why Attend Church?

Reading: Acts 4:23-37

Have you ever heard people say, "I don't have to go to church to be a Christian"? Of course, the statement is true. No one who knows his or her Bible would suggest that a person becomes a Christian by attending church or by participating in its activities. It would be foolish to believe that by going to church and becoming a member someone becomes a child of God.

Sadly, though, that is exactly what many believe, and yet the Bible is very clear on this. A person becomes a Christian by entering into a personal relationship with Jesus Christ the only Saviour. Jesus said:

> *"I am the way and the truth and the life. No one comes to the Father except through me."* (John 14:6)

Such a relationship, however, is much more likely to be entered into if one attends church where the Bible is taught than if he doesn't. A person is also more likely to grow and mature in his or her Christian life if he or she attends church. One doesn't have to attend school in order to be educated. Few achieve a significant education, however, apart from the teaching that is given by an educational institution.

Church services are, or should be, designed to exalt Christ and to strengthen our faith. The church also provides loving fellowship. It binds people together in a spiritual family where there is a genuine care for one another. The church should be a place where parents and children worship God together and fellowship with other believers.

The most valuable gift parents can give to their children is a genuine faith in God. What greater help could a child be given than to know that the Creator and Sustainer of the universe knows him personally, loves him, understands all his anxieties and fears and is ready to help and comfort him in his deepest needs?

The church should be a place for individuals to worship God, learn, be equipped and develop lasting relationships and Christian maturity. Its activities should be designed to bring spiritual richness and blessings to the entire family.

> *After they prayed, the place where they were meeting was shaken. And they were all filled with the Holy Spirit and spoke the Word of God boldly.* (Acts 4:31)

Dear reader, if you have no regular church home, or if you have not yet experienced the warm spiritual family environment of a church you can call your spiritual home, then I would encourage you to find one. Look for a Bible-based church where Jesus is the centre of everything and holiness, service and evangelism are the main preoccupation.

Woe to the Shepherds!
Reading: Jeremiah 23:1-8

When I read, in Jeremiah 23:1, the words: *"'Woe to the shepherds who are destroying and scattering the sheep of my pasture!' declares the Lord,"* a vivid picture of shepherds comes into my mind.

As a teenager, I would spend my summer months with my grandparents who had a business outside Athens, Greece. One of the things I loved to do was watch the sheep graze in the fields. There were different groups of sheep and each group had a master shepherd and other younger shepherds. I was fascinated by the way the master shepherd would lead and protect the sheep, even if he had to risk his life. Just before sunset he would make sure that all of them were there and then he would lead them into the safety of the fold. The devotion of the shepherd to his sheep made a lasting impression on me.

I am sure that God had in mind the good shepherd who is willing to give his life for his sheep when He spoke to the wicked rulers and leaders of Judah. Let's see whether these words apply to us, too:

> *"Woe to the shepherds who are destroying and scattering the sheep of my pasture!" declares the LORD. Therefore this is what the LORD, the God of Israel, says to the shepherds who tend my people: "Because you*

> *have scattered my flock and driven them away and have not bestowed care on them, I will bestow punishment on you for the evil you have done," declares the LORD. "I myself will gather the remnant of my flock out of all the countries where I have driven them and will bring them back to their pasture, where they will be fruitful and increase in number. I will place shepherds over them who will tend them, and they will no longer be afraid or terrified, nor will any be missing," declares the LORD.*
> (Jeremiah 23:1-4)

There are good shepherds and leaders who have dedicated their lives to the Lord and to their flocks and their only aim is to feed and protect those whom they serve. These shepherds have been leading eternal souls to Jesus, the Master Shepherd who gave His life to save the lost. For all these good shepherds we thank God.

Sadly, however, there are many who call themselves pastors or ministers, but all they do is confuse, destroy and scatter the sheep. Some of them may be devoted to their ministry, but they follow a religion of "churchianity", political correctness and interfaith activities. The sheep are entertained and kept busy, but they are spiritually neglected and starving to death.

When Apostle Peter told Jesus three times that he loved Him, Jesus told him the first time, *"Feed my lambs."* The second time He said, *"Take care of my sheep."* The third time Jesus said to Peter, *"Feed my sheep."*

Dear reader, if you are a shepherd or a leader, are you feeding your flock? And if you are a sheep, are you being guided, fed and protected?

Christian Unity
Reading: Acts 2:38-47

The subject of unity in Canada has been a major political preoccupation of most Canadians for as long as I can remember. Nations all over the world are struggling to achieve unity. The strength of our nation depends on how united we are and how peacefully we live with each other.

Similarly, our Christian life and survival depends on our unity with other believers. The expression "strength in numbers" is true if those "numbers" represent one.

> *Then all the Israelites... came out as one man and assembled before the Lord in Mizpah.* (Judges 20:1)

Throughout history, every attempt to create world unity has failed—even limited unions could not survive. Political unions such as the USSR have failed. Religious unions like the ecumenical movement have failed. "Christian unity" does not refer to a worldwide effort to merge all Christian religions under one government and rule. That cannot—and must not—be done. The Bible forbids it.

Rather, Christian unity is a spiritual state in a true believer, manifested in his or her daily life. The Bible clearly teaches that the Christian life is not to be lived alone. There must be togetherness.

> *Can two walk together except they have agreed?* (Amos 3:3)

Certainly not! Life is a journey and it can be very unpleasant when we walk with people whom we do not agree with.

Unity in our Christian life and witness is essential. No wonder the believers in Acts 2 wanted to be together daily.

> *Every day they continued to meet together in the temple courts... with glad and sincere hearts.* (Acts 2:46)

King David said:

> *Glorify the Lord with me; let us exalt His name together.* (Psalm 34:3)

Can you imagine a church worship service where you were the only believer present? You enter alone, pray alone, sing alone and then leave alone. Isn't it clear why "TV church" is not enough for the believer? There is no fellowship! In a true family of believers, one person's pain should become the pain of all the others. One person's joy should become the joy of all the others.

But what is the key to achieving such unity? It is love.

> *My purpose is that they may be encouraged in heart and united in love....* (Colossians 2:2)

Where there is Christian love, there is unity. Without love, Christianity is a farce.

What about your church? Is it...

> *... contending as one man for the faith of the gospel ...?* (Philippians 1:27)

Every church needs committed believers who are united in their desire to serve God. Please consider how *you* can help spread His joy, peace and love.

The Hold-Up

Reading: Exodus 17:1-13

God had helped the Israelites all along their journey. He had given them manna, quail and whatever else they needed to survive. But they continued to complain and murmur—just as we often do. Again, God supplied water to quench their thirst and the children of Israel were refreshed and rejoicing. But, as often happens, trouble followed this blessing: *"The Amalekites came and attacked the Israelites"* (Exodus 17:8).

In this world, we will have trouble and tribulation. Jesus said:

> *"I have told you these things, so that in me you may have peace. In this world you will have trouble. But take heart! I have overcome the world."* (John 16:33)

Once again, the Israelites were in trouble and Moses led his nation to victory, with God's help. Moses asked Joshua to lead a select force into battle, and Moses, Aaron and Hur oversaw the battle from a hill.

What does this battle have to do with the Church? We, in the Church, are also in battle. Our battle is not against governments or other religions or even ourselves, as some may think. Our battle is against the forces of evil that are at war against us (Ephesians 6:10-12).

There are some mistaken ideas about the work and role of the Church, but the truth is:

- We are not here just to preach and teach.
- We are not here just to raise money—no matter what the purpose may be.

- We are not here just to run programs and activities.

According to the Word of God, we are here to do spiritual battle with the enemy—the spiritual forces of evil. We must remember that eternal issues are at stake—not doctrinal and religious traditions and customs. Souls hang in the balance. Basic standards of purity and holiness are being compromised. Foundations of decency are crumbling. Today, right is wrong and wrong is right.

But God has given us the equipment to win the battle: the power of the gospel (Romans 1:16), the power of the Holy Spirit (1 John 4:4), the armour of God (Ephesians 6:13) and, finally, the victory (1 Corinthians 15:57-58).

We may become tired in this battle of life, just as Moses did. What was the secret weapon in the war with Amalek? It was prayer and total dependence on God. When Moses held up his hands—a symbol of appeal to God for help—the Israelites were winning, but when he let his hands down, the Amalekites were winning.

Moses had been told by God in the past to *"stretch his hands to the Lord for help"* (Exodus 9:22). And he had obeyed and experienced God's power. What stands out in this story is that, even though God was there to help the God-fearing Israelites to win and He expected them to completely depend and trust Him, He also expected them to do their part—to pray and to fight.

Sometimes the battles are not won right away and so we get tired and weary and we let our guard down, we stop praying. Moses, too, became very tired. He could not go on alone. He needed help.

Pastors sometimes get tired or weary because of fatigue, whether it relates to the ministry or personal and family matters. Each one of us sometimes fights fatigue. What can we do to help one another to win our battles? We can hold up the hands of those who are weary. In Moses' case, a stone was provided so that he could rest and then Aaron and Hur held up his arms.

How can we "hold up" tired hands? First of all, we can be there when we are needed—ready to help. We must also pray for one another, as Moses prayed for the people in battle; we must refuse to judge and condemn one another; we must faithfully worship with one another; and we must join those who, like Aaron and Hur, are active in the ministry of our Lord.

The battle was won because Aaron and Hur were ready to hold up Moses' hands in prayer all day long. Are we ready and willing to hold up weary and tired hands until we have victory?

We Are Not Alone

Reading: Matthew 4:1-11

People have always been fascinated by stories of invisible, supernatural beings involved in celestial good-versus-evil struggles. Some people claim to have personal "guides" or "channels" who enable them to contact the spirits of the dead. The New Age emphasis on "unseen friends" is part of a world view that has spread all over. Books on channelling, crystals, visualizations, reincarnation and astrology are flooding the market and are being viewed with respect. These ideas have even entered into the classrooms of our schools.

Although we have no solid basis to speak of a New Age "conspiracy", we should recognize that thousands of people today claim that, through hypnosis and mind-altering drugs, they have been able to make genuine contact with spirit beings who become very real to them.

Those who believe in the authority of the Bible should not be surprised by such developments. From cover to cover, the Bible describes the activities of unseen spirits who have a long history of interacting with the human race. The Bible is also clear, however, that the subject of angels should be dealt with cautiously and with discernment. The unseen spirit world can be either harmful or helpful, therefore it must not be treated as an intriguing curiosity but, rather, as an unseen world and society from which we have much to learn.

What can we learn from angels?

WE ARE NOT ALONE

The Bible makes it clear that human beings are not the only intelligent, moral creatures in the universe. The words "angel" and "angels" are found about 300 times in the Bible. The Bible also speaks often about Satan and demons and refers to them as real, though not flesh-and-blood, and earth-bound like us (Ephesians 6:12).

WE ARE HELPED BY UNSEEN FRIENDS

The Bible says that there are angels who help us. These angels are our unseen friends.

> *Are not all angels ministering spirits sent to serve those who will inherit salvation?* (Hebrews 1:14)

Of course, the answer is yes. Angels are normally invisible because they are spirits and they can move quickly from the spirit world to our physical world to help us.

WE ARE OPPOSED BY INVISIBLE ENEMIES

As we study the Bible, we discover that we have enemies in the spirit world. A large number of evil spirits hate God. And this hatred makes these demons do all they can to frustrate

God's purposes for the human race. The Bible refers to the devil as our enemy (1 Peter 5:8; Matthew 13:39) and describes his followers as an organized and powerful army. These demons:

- oppose God and His people
- accuse God and His people
- deceive the unsaved and try to deceive the true believers
- plant evil thoughts into the minds of people
- take over the personality of some people
- influence government leaders
- try to pervert the doctrine of grace
- try to distort the biblical view of Jesus Christ

Knowing what Satan, the enemy, aims to do and how he does it, it can be very scary and discouraging, but it is good and beneficial if we use the information to build a good defence and plan a counter-attack.

The Apostle James gave the following plan:

> *Submit yourselves, then, to God. Resist the devil, and he will flee from you.* (James 4:7)

In a nutshell, victory over evil is possible by first wanting to do God's will and then humbly submitting to Him and resisting the devil in God's strength (Ephesians 6:11-18).

I would like to remind you that those who believe in Jesus Christ and are born-again will stand with

> *… thousands upon thousands of angels in joyful assembly….* (Hebrews 12:22)

Jesus also said:

> *"There is joy in the presence of the angels of God over one sinner who repents."* (Luke 15:10)

If you have questions about the spirit world, don't run to your local bookstore... just read your Bible!

The Christian and the Occult
Reading: Deuteronomy 18:9-13; Isaiah 47:11-15

A national newspaper reported several years ago that the occult was the fastest growing religion. I am not surprised—a large number of questions I am asked deal with the occult and its various forms.

Someone with a spiritual vacuum will look for something to fill it with. Satan offers to help the empty, curious and often gullible person with something out of his workshop. His most powerful tool is the occult.

To many, the word "occult" is vague. The word comes from the Latin *occultus*, which means hidden. In other words, the occult deals with things that are invisible, mysterious and mystical.

The following is a partial list of the different forms of the occult and their descriptions:

SPIRITISM: The belief that one can contact the dead through a medium to receive revelations from the "beyond".

CLAIRVOYANCE: The belief that some people possess extra-sensory perception (ESP), the ability to know or see what others can't.

FORTUNE-TELLING: This includes reading tea leaves, coffee cups, palms, cards, crystal balls, etc.

ASTROLOGY: The belief that the future can be foretold by studying the positions of the heavenly bodies.

HOROSCOPES: Surprised? This is the outgrowth of astrology. Predictions are made based on a chart with the twelve signs of the Zodiac.

WITCHCRAFT: This practice goes back to ancient pagan religions. Using priests and priestesses, rituals and chants, witches claim they are able to contact and use powers from the unseen world.

The Bible forbids involvement with the occult! The devil is using many of his dangerous tools today to trick people into descending the "stairway to hell". Millions of people, including Christians, are unknowingly participating in real occult practices and opening doors for demons to enter their bodies. Unfortunately, many of these people discover the truth only when they have taken the last step down the stairway.

Christians must flee these evil practices!

> *And do not give the devil a foothold.* (Ephesians 4:27)

> *Be very careful, then, how you live—not as unwise but as wise, making the most of every opportunity, because the days are evil. Therefore do not be foolish, but understand what the Lord's will is.* (Ephesians 5:15-17)

Spiritual Separation

Reading: 2 Corinthians 6:14-7:1

If God the Father loved the world and sent His only Son to die on the cross for all mankind; if Jesus the Son gave His own life to save sinners from eternal death and spent more time with sinners than He did with religious leaders; and if we are to make disciples of all nations by bringing the Good News of God's love for mankind… how can we talk about separation from the world?

A careful look at the Word of God will help us understand the meaning and spirit of pronouncements such as *"Do not be yoked together with unbelievers"* and *"Come out from them and be separate"* and God's words spoken through Isaiah:

> *Depart, depart, go out from there!… you who carry the vessels of the Lord.* (Isaiah 52:11)

Let's look at the phrase *"unequally yoked"*. In Deuteronomy 22:10 we read, *"Do not plough with an ox and a donkey yoked together."* Why not? Because the ox was a clean animal while the donkey was unclean, and their step and pull were different. In contrast, a Christian finds that Jesus' yoke *"is easy and His burden is light"* (Matthew 11:29-30).

The reference in 2 Corinthians is clear that believers should separate themselves from wickedness, darkness, Satan (Belial), idols and those who practise and live in them. This includes marriage and business relationships. A true Christian should not go into partnership with an unsaved person. How can one who is faithful to Christ consistently go on in a partnership where the name of Jesus is unwelcome?

The instructions also apply to our daily social lives. Of course, a Christian should be in contact with the unsaved and make every effort to bring the Good News of Jesus Christ to them, but we should never join them in their sinful activities in such a way as to seem no different from them.

We must also follow this guideline in so-called religious activities and practices. So many "Christian" activities are anything but. One that stands out is Halloween. While the day has come to be known as a fun occasion to dress up and go "trick or treating", it remains a time when morals, modesty, spirituality and restraints are all but forgotten.

There isn't enough space here to go into the background of Halloween, which is clearly rooted in Satanism, but let me ask you: when our children dress up in costumes, when we put up scary-looking decorations or allow our children to be entertained by haunted houses, what are we doing? Are we not compromising our stand as Christians?

The Bible says:

> *Have nothing to do with the fruitless deeds of darkness, but rather expose them. For it is shameful even to mention what the disobedient do in secret.* (Ephesians 5:11-12)

Power over Satan
Reading: Mark 5:1-20

One day a woman called me and asked, "Do you pray for demon-possessed people? I am demon possessed." Although I had received all kinds of calls from people who claimed to have multiple personalities or be possessed by evil spirits, and a few who had threatened me while they were under the influence of satanic powers, this particular call gave me the shivers.

She told me about the powers that had been given to her by her mother and grandmother, both priestesses who were practising witchcraft. To make a very long story short, after many prayers and a period of calmness, she started coming to church and prayer meetings.

One night, right after the Bible study, she asked me to pray with her because she felt the evil spirits in her were trying to destroy her. I asked an elder to come with me into my office to pray with me for her. This woman reminded me of the demon-possessed man in the New Testament who lived in the tombs and could not be controlled, even with chains. She screamed and shouted, started foaming and turned red hot. When I touched her arm it felt like burning coal. With God's help, and through Jesus Christ, she was delivered.

The Bible says that a large number of those whom Jesus healed were *"possessed by demons."* What or who were these demons?

In the Gospels, demons are described as belonging to the kingdom of Satan, with knowledge that Jesus is the Son of God. They spoke, recognizing that they had a separate personality and consciousness than the person in whom they dwelt. These spirits were waiting to be tormented in the abyss and looked ahead to the judgment with fear and trembling.

Jesus was not interested in the demons but in the people who suffered because of them. The Bible is clear that demoniacs were not mere lunatics but real cases of *"invaded personalities"*. The demons, whatever their origin or nature, were evil and afflicted the many people they entered.

In Mark 5:1-20, Christ met His (and our) enemy in a graveyard. Here was a dangerous and wild man, possessed by a legion of demons—enough to drive 2,000 pigs to drown in a lake. These demons recognized the authority of Jesus Christ immediately. They preferred to live in swine rather than go to their own place.

As Christians, we must face the reality that demonic powers are real and are here to stay until the judgment day. Every Christian has a fight to fight, a struggle against the powers of darkness.

> *For our struggle is not against flesh and blood, but against the rulers, against the authorities, against the powers of this dark world and against the spiritual forces of evil in the heavenly realms.* (Ephesians 6:12)

Satan wants to destroy our bodies and condemn our souls to hell. The fact that the demons were afraid that Christ would *"torture them before their time"* (Matthew 8:29) indicates that there is a future judgment for Satan and his armies. Demons need bodies in order to do their work in this world, just as the Holy Spirit needs the Christian's Body.

While Satan still uses demon possession to express his hatred for God and mankind, he usually does so in less spectacular ways. For example, he might get people to believe that, if there is God, He won't mind people having fun and pleasure, even if it seems immoral and sinful to fanatics.

Such a belief is very attractive to many because it promises freedom from moral restraints and offers immediate gratification. But many who start down that road of permissiveness are soon trapped in a lifestyle of addiction and shameless practices that rob them of self-respect, satisfaction and hope. And, actually, Satan has them in his power, just as he had the demon-possessed man in his power.

We should be encouraged in knowing that Christ has power over Satan.

> *You, dear children, are from God and have overcome them, because the one who is in you is greater than the one who is in the world.* (1 John 4:4)

And He gives us the authority to fight the enemy:

> *Submit yourselves, then, to God. Resist the devil and he will flee from you.* (James 4:7)

The good news for those who are trapped in sin is that Jesus Christ still delivers all who turn to Him. And the good news for those who have trusted Christ for deliverance is that we have a message of hope that is worth telling!

Will you tell others about Jesus and His saving power?

The Real Enemy

Reading: Revelation 3

Our real enemy today is not a world full of sin and unrighteousness. Our battles are not against the world and its corrupt system. Yes, there is a lot of corruption and sin around us—we live *"in the midst of a crooked and perverse generation"* (Philippians 2:15)—but the real battle today is within the Church.

The sin that is effectively weakening and destroying the Church and its testimony and influence is the sin of apathy or lukewarmness.

> *"So, because you are lukewarm—neither hot nor cold—I am about to spit you out of my mouth."* (Revelation 3:16)

Lukewarmness is spiritual paralysis. It is forsaking one's first love (Revelation 2:4). It is the gradual loss of zeal (Psalm 69:9). Jesus said:

> *"You have a reputation of being alive, but you are dead."* (Revelation 3:1)

Lukewarmness means less service, less prayer (or none at all), satisfaction with spiritual "bare necessities", self-centredness and self-righteousness. It also means giving grudgingly or not at all, thus robbing God.

> *Will a man rob God? Yet you rob me. But you ask, "How do we robe you?" In tithes and offerings.* (Malachi 3:8)

Lukewarmness also indicates lack of a spirit of evangelism, but plenty of desire for entertainment and the popular sport of doctrinal and denominational competition. Lukewarmness is another evil and dangerous satanic plan of deception. That's why it is so dangerous: the devil does not destroy all the doctrinal truths. That would be too obvious. While Satan is deceiving people into believing that everything is fine, religious leaders are busy with religious activities and doctrinal wars.

The victim, not understanding his real condition, feels good and satisfied just the way he is and he remains in that condition. He does not see the need to change. He feels very proud of his religion, but he does not realize that, in the eyes of God he is pitiful, poor, blind and naked (Revelation 3:17). He is religious, but his religion is an abomination to God.

Is there a cure for lukewarmness? Of course there is! The cure is given by Jesus Himself:

> *"I counsel you to buy from me gold refined in the fire, so you can become rich; and white clothes to wear, so you can cover your shameful nakedness; and salve to put on your eyes, so you can see."* (Revelation 3:18)

How long will we remain idle and lukewarm? What is keeping us idle and apathetic, even though we see the Church being threatened with spiritual paralysis and destruction? How can we remain idle while the world is going through such a frightening crisis? Soon it may be too late.

Pray, dear believer, pray!

> *Precious Lord, have mercy on us. Revive Your Church; revive me today, Lord. Help Your Church turn away from sin and walk in holiness. Lord, purify Your Church!*

Revival!

Reading: Psalm 85

"Revival" is a very misunderstood word—often used, but more often misused. A revival is more than just a series of religious meetings or services. In fact, the word revival is used in the secular world as well as in the religious, especially in the field of medicine, to describe a particular change.

Let's look at the dictionary definition of the word "revive": bring or come back to life, vigour, use, etc. In the business world, "revive" may mean bringing something back into style, for example. In religion, revival usually refers to an awakening or increase of interest in religion, or special services or efforts to bring about this renewed interest.

But what is the biblical and spiritual meaning of the word "revive"?

> *Will you not revive us again, that your people may rejoice in you?* (Psalm 85:6)

Revival has to do with bringing back life and specifically describes a spiritual change.

Obviously, revival is only needed when somebody is about to die or is unconscious, when the spirit is gone or almost gone… and this would apply to a church body as well. The result of a revived church is a fruitful life. This kind of revival can be the experience of the whole Body of Christ, a local church or an individual Christian. Revival is the process of bringing or coming back to life or consciousness. However, any revival that is not based on God's Word will be like a skyrocket, which goes up with a great flash and comes down as a stick.

The psalmist prayed for revival: *"Will you not revive us again?"* All revival begins with prayer! Prayer is the wire that connects us to the power source. D.L. Moody said, "Every great work of God can be traced to a kneeling figure." God said:

> *If my people, who are called by my name, will humble themselves and pray and seek my face and turn from their wicked ways, then will I hear from heaven and will forgive their sin and heal their land.* (2 Chronicles 7:14)

To pray for revival, we must first understand what revival is and what it does to an individual or a church. We must determine whether we or our churches need and want to be revived. The person or church that has compromised and allowed sin to come in and take away the first love needs revival. The person or church that has fallen asleep spiritually needs revival.

Revival and rejoicing go hand in hand—*"Will you not revive us again, that your people may rejoice in you?"* Love dominates all true revivals and is always active in kindness. Revival helps people focus on Jesus rather than on religion or the corrupt world system. Revival does not take away your life—on the contrary, revival brings life and joy! When a revival starts in one person, others are sure to join in.

Are you willing to let a revival begin in you?

The Valley of Dry Bones
Reading: Ezekiel 37:1-14

About 600 years before the birth of Christ, God gave the prophet Ezekiel a vision that was full of power and symbolism. This vision had two basic messages.

The first message was regarding the nation of Israel and the second was regarding the human race in general. To the nation of Israel—which was defeated, torn apart and scattered around the world—the message brought a prediction of a national resurrection and reunion. Politically, this took place on May 14, 1948, when the modern Israel officially became a nation.

Sadly, however, the nation is still spiritually dead today. Yet the Bible says that one day, when Jesus Christ returns, the nation of Israel will turn to Jesus and be saved (Romans 11:25-26).

Although this vision applies mainly to the Jews, it is also clear that it applies to the Christian covenant and the general resurrection of the dead (John 5:28-29). The term "Israel" in the New Testament, although used of Jews, sometimes applies to Christians (Galatians 3:8-9).

Here, we will look at the second message of this vision—that of the lost world in general. We live in a world dead in sin. Even though we see people everywhere, moving and walking and doing things, spiritually speaking, most of them are dryer than dry bones found in a desert.

Without God's intervention, this world would have remained just that… a valley of dry bones without any hope of a present or future life. But God did intervene. God's Spirit is always at work and He wants to impress us, just as He impressed Ezekiel, of the need of revival.

It probably took Ezekiel a while, walking around in the valley, to see the need for—and then believe in the possibility of—a revival. Often, lack of faith prevents revivals.

God tests our faith before His Spirit works through us. He asked Ezekiel, *"Can these bones live?"* Ezekiel's answer was careful and noncommittal: *"I don't know, Lord."* God wanted Ezekiel to speak to the dry bones and give them an important message, so He urged Ezekiel to simply obey His instructions and then trust Him to do the rest.

Ezekiel reluctantly preached the Word of God to the lifeless skeletons. Before he was even finished, they began to rattle and come together and muscles and skin grew on them. A few more words and the bodies came to life.

Ezekiel believed God and obeyed His commands—and the mass of dry bones turned into a vast army. If you ever feel like you are talking to dry bones, simply share the Good News from the Word of God and He will take care of the rest.

A revival is possible! God's Spirit brings life. This thrilling truth is needed in this world. We need the Holy Spirit to come with His changing power and revive us all. As the body without breath is dead, so is the person or church without the Holy Spirit dead.

You are in a valley of dry bones. How will you respond?

You've Been Warned!
Reading: Ezekiel 33:1-20

When the water supply of a town in Ontario became contaminated with deadly bacteria called E. coli, hundreds of people became very sick and many died. People panicked, wanting to know if they had been infected. To prevent this deadly bacterium from infecting the rest of the population, the city officials, the government and the people in general started a vigorous campaign to warn people of the impending danger.

When things seemed to be under control, the finger pointing started. Some government officials were blamed for this tragedy. They were accused of doing nothing to warn the public, even though they had been informed and warned about the contamination of the water supply months before the outbreak. People complained that if they had been warned, so many lives would not have been lost and the rest would have been spared agony, pain and the fear of death.

However, according to the news, the warnings had been ignored and the unsuspecting public went on with their lives as if everything was fine. That is, of course, until people started dying. Then the common cry was: "I wish someone had warned us!"

The same cry will be heard one day when a countless number of people stand before the judgement throne. Each individual will give an account for ignoring the warnings of the Bible. But, according to the Word of God, it will be too late then.

> *Just as man is destined to die once, and after that to face judgement....* (Hebrews 9:27)

Just as everyone who was infected by the E. coli bacteria had to be treated to wash away the deadly bacteria from their bodies, so it is with the human heart and soul, which is infected by the deadly sin that kills. It needs to be washed and disinfected, and the only thing that can do this is the blood of Jesus Christ that was shed on the cross.

But people have to be warned and God uses believers to do the job. He makes it very clear in His Word:

> *When I say to the wicked, "O wicked man, you will surely die," and you do not speak out to dissuade him from his ways, that wicked man will die for his sin, and I will hold you accountable for his blood.* (Ezekiel 33:8)

Jesus gave us clear instructions. The last words of Jesus before he went to heaven were:

> *"Go make disciples of all nations, baptizing them in the name of the Father and of the Son and of the Holy Spirit."* (Matthew 28:19)

To ignore God's warnings and to fail to warn others of the imminent danger of eternal death is like knowing that your city's water supply is contaminated with deadly bacteria and not warning your family members and others of the danger. Do you know the dangers of spiritual contamination? Have you been washed with the blood of Jesus and are you warning others?

Why?

Reading: John 9

When people face tragic circumstances they usually look for explanations. I remember a mother who had just been informed that her four children, her husband and her son-in-law had been killed in a terrible car accident. After the initial shock and the cry, "Why Lord?" she turned to those around her and said, "The Lord gave them to me and the Lord took them away. Glory to His name."

Questions like "Why?", "Why me?" and "Why now?" have no easy answers. Often we volunteer answers or explanations about tragic events, without thinking about the effects of our words. I have heard people blame God, the parents of a sick child, or the lack of faith of a person who is very sick or who cannot find a job and so on.

This was the attitude of the disciples when they saw a blind man and asked Jesus, *"Rabbi, who sinned, this man or his parents, that he was born blind?"* Many believed the blindness was punishment for sin, either his or his parents'. But let's look at Jesus' reply:

> *"Neither this man nor his parents sinned... but this happened so that the work of God might be displayed in his life."* (John 9:3)

Why is there so much bad news in the world today? The Bible has the answer to that question: This is a fallen world, corrupted by sin and dominated by Satan. The goal of Satan and his angels is to corrupt and destroy whatever and whomever they can.

But let's not stop there! There is also good news in the world today. God has intervened by sending His Son Jesus to break the power of sin and purify for Himself a people that are His very own (Titus 2:14). Through His people, God wants to demonstrate His power and glory in good times and in bad times.

Dear reader, will you volunteer to be that kind of an example and object lesson to those around you today?

Invite Them to Church

Reading: Matthew 9:9-13

Peter left his house for church one Sunday just as his next-door neighbour was loading his golf clubs into his car. "Good morning, Bob," the neighbour called. "Come and play golf with me today." Bob answered firmly, "No, thank you. I am Christian and I always go to church on Sundays."

After a long pause the golfer said, "You know, Bob, I have often wondered about you and your church and I really admire your faithfulness. I have invited you to play golf with me so many times, but you have never once invited me to go to church with you."

What a shocker that was for Bob. And what an eye-opener! This message is for all the "Bobs" in today's churches.

Jesus challenges us all today as he challenged the Pharisees in His day.

> *"I desire mercy, not sacrifice. For I have not come to call the righteous, but sinners."* (Matthew 9:13)

In other words, God's desire is not to see us merely practise our religion and occasionally thank Him for our salvation. Rather, He wants us to show mercy and love to those who need salvation.

Do we really care about the people around us? Have you ever thought of the destiny of people without Christ? Many are dying daily without Christ… some of them you know. But there are many more who are still alive. We are surrounded by people who are without Christ.

I am sure there are many around you that have never been invited to meet Jesus. I hope the story of "Bob" and his neighbour will stir you to compassion greater than your comfortable routine of practising religion or your fear of rejection.

Pray for the families and people around you. Ask God to help you love them and to give you the courage to speak to them about the love of God and about what Jesus did on the cross for our salvation… and what He will do for them if they invite Him into their lives.

And invite them to church.

"We Found Him!"

Reading: John 1:40-51

For many years now I have been helping John Ertsos, the Greek evangelist, by maintaining his three-minute message phone line that people can call to hear the gospel in Greek. Several years ago, I was listening to the messages that people had left on the answering machine when the voice of an elderly woman made me hold my breath.

She was crying desperately and repeating: "I am old and alone, all alone. Can anyone please, please help me?" Without leaving her name or phone number, she hung up. She called twice after that, the third time exclaiming, "I have been looking for someone to help me—not materially, but spiritually! Oh, Blessed Virgin Mary, can anyone help me?" She was searching for someone to help her, but I couldn't do anything. She never identified herself.

A few days later I got a phone call and this time we knew the young woman. She had called to say "Thank you" and "Good bye". She had taken a bottle of pills and she was going to die. Why? She was hurting, lonely and desperate. This time we were able to help. When the ambulance reached her, she was already unconscious but, with God's help, she survived.

People everywhere are crying out, "Who can help me find some peace and joy in life? To whom should I go?" Even Apostle Peter asked,

> "Lord, to whom shall we go? You have the words of eternal life. We believe and know that you are the Holy One of God." (John 6:68-69)

King David said:

> Taste and see that the Lord is good. (Psalm 34:8)

But how can people "taste" God unless someone brings them to Him? If you have tasted the Lord, should you keep it a secret?

The first thing Andrew did was find his brother, Simon, and give him the good news:

> "We have found the Messiah...." (John 1:41)

Then he brought his brother to Jesus and Jesus changed

Simon's name to Peter. Philip found Nathaniel and invited him to come, saying,

> "We have found… Jesus of Nazareth… come and see…." (John 1:45-46)

An unbeliever was heard saying, "If I believed in all the things you Christians believe in, like heaven and hell, eternity and life after death… I would stand in the middle of the street and yell, 'Stop! Stop all of you and turn to Jesus or else you will be lost forever!'"

We do the bringing. God does the rest. The person you bring to Christ might be prepared and ready to be a great spiritual leader, but you must still do your part. God knows each of us, but He does not force His way into our lives. We must make Him our God and King.

Coffee Break

Just a Spark

Who would ever remember a small spark?
Yet who could forget a forest fire started by that same spark?

I am just a tiny spark,
flickering for a moment and then disappearing... forever!
Yet a tiny spark like me is all it takes to start a forest fire.

Just a spark, you say?
Yes, but "just a spark" can get a fireplace blazing,
a furnace working,
a lamp burning,
a candle glowing,
a car running.

Yes, just a spark.
But imagine a world without sparks!

A spark can be the beginning of good or of bad...
or it can be wasted.
What kind of spark will you be?

Not Me, Lord

Reading: Exodus 3:1-15; 4:10-17

When Moses went out with his sheep one morning, it seemed like any other day he had spent tending his flock. But it was to be a special day. Moses was going to meet God. We must always be ready because we never know what God has planned for each one of us.

God appeared to Moses and revealed His glory through the burning bush. Then, when God called Moses, he responded, "Here I am." It was as if he expected to hear God's voice. Are we sensitive to God's voice in even the most unlikely places and situations?

God is a living and loving God, full of compassion and ready to help.

> *"I have... seen the misery.... I have heard them crying... I am concerned.... I have come to rescue them!"* (Exodus 3:7-8)

What a message of grace! What a wonderful God! He sees, He hears, He cares, He rescues. But He usually uses people like you and me. And so, God called Moses for service. He said,

> *"So now, go, I am sending you!"* (Exodus 3:10)

God had prepared Moses for eighty years for the job and now was the time. Unfortunately, Moses did not reply, "Here am I, Lord. Send me!" Instead, he questioned God. He tried four different arguments against God's will for his life.

First, he asked, "Who am I?" Forty years of training and discipline in the desert as a shepherd had humbled him, but he had also become very comfortable in what he was doing. God wanted Moses to be a greater shepherd and lead his nation out of bondage and into the Promised Land. He even reassured him of His presence:

"I will be with you." (Exodus 3:12)

Still Moses doubted.

His second argument was that the Jews would want to know by what authority Moses was asking them to move to an unknown place. So God patiently revealed His name, Jehovah. *"I AM who I AM"*

Moses' third argument was, "What if they do not believe me?" God had told him that they would believe him so Moses' statement only showed his own unbelief.

In a final attempt to get out of the job God had for him, Moses complained: *"O Lord, I have never been eloquent, neither in the past nor since you have spoken to your servant. I am slow of speech and tongue"* (Exodus 4:10). Moses was looking at himself and his weaknesses instead of looking at God and His power.

God assured Moses:

"I will help you speak and will teach you what to say." (Exodus 4:12)

Moses still didn't get it and he pleaded with God to find someone else for the job. God did almost everything for Moses, short of doing the work Himself, but Moses still refused!

Although God became angry with Moses, He did not walk away. He gave him Aaron, his brother, as a helper (but Aaron turned out to be a hindrance rather than a help).

We are all called to serve God—perhaps not to lead a nation, but a group of only two or three. Maybe it's to sing in the choir or dust pews. God wants our availability, not our ability. What is your answer: "Here I am. Send me!" or "Not me, Lord. Send someone else"?

The New Life

Reading: Acts 5

The apostles had a mission and nothing would stop them from accomplishing it. In Acts 5 we see them and all the believers filled with the Holy Spirit and united.

The apostles performed many miraculous signs and wonders and, as a result, many people accepted the Good News and were added to their number. However, the high priest and his associates had the apostles arrested and put in jail. The religious leaders had warned them not to ever preach or talk about Jesus, but the apostles were not intimidated or afraid to tell people about Jesus and they ended up in jail.

"That should teach them a lesson," the priests probably thought. But they had forgotten God. How can anyone or anything stop God, or prevent Him from accomplishing His mission? God sent an angel and the apostles were freed.

And God sent a message. Actually, it was an order:

> *Go, stand in the temple courts... and tell the people the full message of this new life.* (Acts 5:20)

Was this for real? Was God actually ordering them to go back to the place they had been arrested and preach?

Well, those may have been our questions, but not theirs.

> *At daybreak they entered the temple courts, as they had been told, and began to teach the people.* (Acts 5:21)

Nothing would stop the apostles and the believers from spreading the Good News of this new life that Jesus had brought—not even prison or threats of death. They had decided to follow Jesus… no matter what.

What about us today? Are we willing to talk about Jesus and the new life that He gives, no matter what the cost may be? Or are we intimidated and embarrassed?

The same order is given to us too: *"Go and tell all the people about the new life."* Are you willing to obey?

Good News
Reading: Acts 14:8-20

There are many people who use the word "gospel" regularly without really knowing its true meaning. The Greek word for gospel is *"evaggelion"* which simply means "good news" or a "good message". The "Good News" is a message that, when heard for the first time, excites another person.

The Apostle Paul described this message, this Good News, over and over in the book of Acts. For example, while Paul and Barnabas were in Lystra (a city in present-day Turkey), they explained the gospel this way:

> *We are bringing you good news, telling you to turn from these worthless things to the living God….* (Acts 14:15)

The good news that Paul had for them was that they did not have to trust the worthless idols and things that they had been serving. They could give their lives to a living God—the One who was powerful enough to create the world and loving enough to care for them. And you know what? Many believed this good news and changed their way of life.

I believe the world has not changed much. People are still

serving "worthless things" but, instead of calling them idols, we call them jobs, money, entertainment, religion, etc. People live lonely, purposeless lives. They often choose worthless things because they do not know what else will work.

And while people are searching to find some good news and a purpose for life, religious people are busy doing their own thing and have their personal agendas. It seems that believers and churches don't really know, or have forgotten, what the gospel of Jesus Christ is all about. We must go back to the Bible and carefully listen to the words of Jesus Christ whose name we bear and then take another good, hard look at our Christianity the way it is being practised today, before it is too late!

Am I—are you—living the "Good News"? Are you really sharing the Good News with your friends, in order to draw them to Jesus? Do you talk to others about God and what He has done to your life? If you bring the Good News, the gospel of Jesus Christ, to those you meet daily, people will respond today as they did many years ago.

Remember: God has saved you and has given meaning to your life. Now, please go and share this Good News with others!

Scripture Reading Index

Genesis 29	183
Exodus 3:1-15	252
Exodus 4:10-17	252
Exodus 17:1-13	228
Deuteronomy 18:9-13	233
Joshua 24:14-27	92
Psalm 8	30, 177
Psalm 23	126
Psalm 32	67, 73
Psalm 34	158
Psalm 42	157, 197
Psalm 51:1-12	26
Psalm 71	155
Psalm 85	241
Proverbs 31	181
Ecclesiastes 1:12-2:11	129
Ecclesiastes 3	141
Ecclesiastes 11:7-12:14	149
Isaiah 5:8-30	176
Isaiah 9:2-7	50
Isaiah 40:28-31	103

Reference	Page
Isaiah 47:11-15	233
Jeremiah 23:1-8	224
Ezekiel 33:1-20	244
Ezekiel 37:1-14	242
Joel 2:12-27	187
Joel 2:12-32	68
Matthew 4:1-11	230
Matthew 5:17-20	41
Matthew 6:1-6	203
Matthew 6:5-15	134
Matthew 7:7-12	143
Matthew 7:28-8:4	166
Matthew 9:1-8	79
Matthew 9:9-13	247
Matthew 9:14-17	199
Matthew 9:18-38	79
Matthew 16:21-28	131
Matthew 18:21-35	71
Matthew 19:16-30	219
Matthew 22:1-14	35
Matthew 23	192
Matthew 23:13-18	203
Matthew 28	217
Mark 5:1-20	236
Mark 5:21-34	28
Mark 9:42-50	168
Mark 12:41-44	206

Luke 2:1-20	48
Luke 2:8-20	47
Luke 2:25-38	47
Luke 4:14-30	207
Luke 6:46-49	124
Luke 7:36-50	66
Luke 9:18-27	137
Luke 9:57-62	110
Luke 10:25-37	37
Luke 13:1-9	76
John 1	44
John 1:40-51	248
John 4:1-42	57
John 5:1-15	133
John 5:31-47	196
John 8:1-12	64, 164
John 9	246
John 14	85
John 21:1-19	90
Acts 2:38-47	226
Acts 4:23-37	222
Acts 4:31-33	214
Acts 5	254
Acts 14:8-20	255
Acts 17:16-34	210
Acts 19	171
Acts 22	39

Reference	Page
Acts 26	42
Romans 3:21-31	188
Romans 3:22-26	59
Romans 5:1-11	118, 160
Romans 8	63
Romans 12	89
1 Corinthians 1	209
1 Corinthians 1:18-31	33
1 Corinthians 2:14-3:4	112
1 Corinthians 13	179
2 Corinthians 4:7-18	31
2 Corinthians 6:14-7:1	169, 234
2 Corinthians 8:1-15	204
Galatians 1:1-9	117
Galatians 5:16-26	117, 139
Ephesians 2:1-10	25
Ephesians 4:7-16	101
Ephesians 5:1-21	109, 173
Philippians 1	83, 140
Philippians 3:7-21	122
Philippians 3:12-16	151
Colossians 1:15-23	220
Colossians 3:1-17	174
Colossians 4:1-17	55
1 Thessalonians 4	81
1 Thessalonians 5:12-28	201
2 Timothy 1	105

2 Timothy 3 152
2 Timothy 4:1-8 136
Titus 3....................................... 120
Hebrews 5:11-6:3 98
Hebrews 6:1-12................................. 154
James 1...................................... 144
James 2:14-26 120
James 5:13-20 77
1 Peter 1:3-25 114
1 Peter 1:13-25 163
1 Peter 2:1-12................................... 99
1 Peter 4:12-19 147
2 Peter 1:3-10................................. 162
2 Peter 3....................................... 96
1 John 1:5-6:11................................ 107
1 John 3:11-24 190
Revelation 3 239
Revelation 3:1-6................................ 212
Revelation 3:14-22............................... 54
Revelation 22:7-21............................... 94